THE
SWEET POISON
QUIT PLAN
COOKBOOK

THE SWEET POISON QUIT PLAN COOKBOOK

DAVID GILLESPIE

PHOTOGRAPHY BY BEN DEARNLEY

VIKING
an imprint of
PENGUIN BOOKS

INTRODUCTION

Sugar makes you fat and, if you consume it for long enough, it will kill you. It is converted directly to fat by your liver and it destroys your body's ability to control your appetite. Without a functioning appetite control you will want to eat more of everything and no amount of dieting or willpower will change that. The more sugar you eat, the fatter you will probably be. But that will be the least of your worries.

Looking unpleasant in work-out gear won't kill you (although it might cause blindness in passers-by), but the metabolic effects of sugar consumption will. Even if you've managed to control your weight, you haven't escaped; you've just avoided the most obvious symptom. Some high-quality studies now confirm that sugar consumption leads straight down a path to fatty liver disease, then insulin resistance, PCOS (Polycystic Ovarian Syndrome), Type II Diabetes and on to depression, anxiety and ultimately dementia. Other studies tell us sugar is responsible for high blood pressure, chronic kidney failure, premature aging, infertility and gout. Even worse than that, it's as addictive as nicotine and embedded in almost everything you eat. So, no matter how much you want to stop eating it, you won't be able to, unless you break that addiction first. Yes, sugar will make you fatter today (and rot your teeth), but give it a few decades and it may well end your life in any one of a long list of unpleasant ways.

The detailed evidence behind all of those alarming statements is contained in my books *Sweet Poison* and *The Sweet Poison Quit Plan*. But this book is not about disease or evidence – it's about fun. It's about still having treats even though you have thrown out the sugar. It's about having something to feed your sugar-addicted guests and having something to put in the school lunch-box. It's about not missing out.

Table sugar (sucrose) is half glucose and half fructose. The glucose half is critically important to our survival. We are a machine that runs on a fuel of pure glucose. Every cell in our body uses it for energy and it is the only fuel our brain can use at all. Don't worry that you're missing out on glucose if you don't eat sugar, as almost every food we eat is ultimately converted to glucose by our efficient fuel extraction system. Glucose is a perfectly normal and necessary part of our diet. It is the fructose half that causes all the destruction and disease. So when I say you're about to cook without sugar, I mean the fructose half of sugar. While chemically dextrose (the commercial name for glucose) is also a sugar, when I use the word 'sugar' I mean the stuff you sprinkle on your cereal, scientifically known as sucrose.

There are plenty of alternative sweeteners I could have used instead of sugar. Natvia (Stevia and Erythritol) and Splenda (sucralose) are two of the more popular sugar alternatives being promoted to bakers, and you will find them in a lot of commercial sugar-free foods. While these sweeteners have been approved for use in Australia, they haven't jumped all the scientific hurdles. It is because they are relatively new in our food supply and there is sufficient scientific caution about their long term safety that I decided to avoid them. Not because I know there is anything wrong with them (I don't), just because I believe the evidence is not clear enough yet to make that call.

If there is anything my reading on hormone and endocrine systems has taught me, it is that we are exquisitely adapted to a very specific set of chemicals found in our environment in very specific quantities and ratios. So it made sense to follow the more challenging (from a cooking perspective) route of trying to use a product that I knew for certain we were chemically adapted to: glucose. Cooking without fructose can present a bit of challenge because it is primarily the fructose half that makes sugar – that is, table sugar – (and the foods made from it) sweet.

This book provides recipes for many popular fructose-replacement foods. It is not about how to make meals that are obviously sugar-free (like bacon and eggs); rather, it is a guide to making sweet foods that can satisfy without the risk of re-addiction to sugar, using dextrose (as well as glucose syrup and rice malt syrup) as the sweetener. These are recipes for you to use to make special treats for the rest of your life.

The recipes in my book *The Sweet Poison Quit Plan* were developed by a mum (my wife, Lizzie) and designed for everyday use (things like the tea cake on page 59 and others you'll recognise if you've read that book). A few of these recipes are included here, but most of the recipes were developed by Peta Dent. Peta is a proper chef, so the recipes are full-on, professionally developed desserts and sweet treats fit for inclusion in any TV chef's collection. This doesn't mean they're hard to make or use bizarre ingredients (Guatamalan chia seeds anyone?).

Peta has cooked each of the recipes dozens of times, trying different combinations and adjusting the quantities until we (and a random selection of sugar-addicted and sugar-free guinea pigs) were happy with the end product. I've tasted all of them. The quality control was hard work, but someone had to battle through all that ice cream and cake (okay, I had a little help from the kids!). Lizzie has also made a lot the recipes to make sure an average person in an average kitchen with an average supermarket down the road can pull them off. They're spectacularly good and we are very excited by the sheer abundance of high-quality fructose-free options this book represents.

So you've shelled out serious money for a chef-developed cookbook and that's what you've got, except that everything between these pages is designed to be safe for recovering sugar-holics.

SOME IMPORTANT NOTES ABOUT DEXTROSE:

- The dextrose that is referred to in most of the recipes is dextrose monohydrate. You can buy it in 1kg bags from the home-brew section of your local supermarket (I can buy it in my local Woolworths for about $3, but at the time of publication Coles don't stock it). It is pure glucose. If your supermarket doesn't have dextrose, hunt down a home-brew supplies shop. Home brewers use dextrose to make beer and their haunts often have industrial quantities available. Dextrose looks like icing sugar, but it's only a little bit sweet and it fizzes slightly on the tongue. (It reminds me of the lemon sherbet I used to consume on my way home from school.) Some recipes use glucose syrup or rice malt syrup, which are liquid forms of glucose.

- Dextrose will taste sweeter and sweeter the further you get into withdrawal from your fructose addiction (see *The Sweet Poison Quit Plan* for details on managing the withdrawal phase). If you taste it while you are still addicted to sugar (go on, dive in – you know you want to!), it will taste almost flour-like, but once you are a month or two past your addiction, it will taste almost as sweet as you remember sugar tasting. This can present a bit of a quandary to a recipe developer. Who is the audience – sugar-addicted folk or sugar-free folk? It takes enormous skill to create food that suits both crowds, and I think Peta has managed it magnificently.

- Dextrose weighs about half as much as sugar, but it takes up more fluid than the equivalent amount of sugar, and seems to burn at a lower temperature. Most of these recipes started life as a normal sugar-based recipe. In substituting dextrose for sugar, Peta (like Lizzie before her) generally increased the ratio of wet ingredients (or decreased the dry ingredients, including the dextrose) until the end product tasted close to the real thing. For good measure, we kept a stable of tame sugarholics on tap to try out the end result. Some recipes (such as the ice creams, pecan pie, chocolate profiteroles and caramel sandwich biscuits) would fool any sugar addict. Un-iced cakes and biscuits (that tasted very sweet to Lizzie and me) were declared bland by the sugar-eaters (in comparison to the full-sugar version), so it might be a good idea to generally keep those for fructose-free folk.

- Dextrose also reduces the shelf-life of the end product if it is a dry food (like cakes and biscuits). A dextrose-based cake will not last as long as its sugar equivalent and most are best eaten within a day of making them. When just made, they are scrumptious, but after a day or two at room temperature, they seem to become too moist and a little sticky, especially if you live in a more humid climate. (They last longer in the fridge.)

The biscuits last a little longer and can be used in school lunch-boxes for at least a week, although they may not maintain their initial crispness. Many of the recipes freeze very well, so Lizzie will often cook up a batch of school-lunch-type treats, portion, and wrap them in plastic film, then freeze them for easy dispensing when needed. There's nothing like a warm school bag to thaw a dextrose cake by morning tea time.

Many thousands of people now live without fructose and most of them say that once they are a year or so into their new life, they no longer have the urge to eat sweets (whether made with dextrose or not). But most of them still have kids to feed, birthday parties to throw and guests to have over to morning tea.

The idea behind this book is to provide solutions for those occasions. If your sweet-toothed mother-in-law is descending next Tuesday you will find a cake and ice cream recipe in this book you can share (without fear of re-addiction) that she will love just as much as the 'real' thing. If you need to throw a party for grade 6, the birthday party recipes will keep things humming along without endangering the health of your own kids. And if your kids threaten mutiny when you announce Easter has been cancelled, there's a section devoted to treats to keep a bunny happy.

In short, this is a cookbook that allows you to be 'normal' in a fructose-addicted world, but, remember this warning:

Do not regularly eat foods sweetened with dextrose (glucose) until you have completed withdrawal from sugar.

It's only once you remove fructose from your diet that dextrose (glucose) becomes a viable alternative to sugar. Consuming it while fructose is wreaking havoc with your appetite control and hormone levels and circulating fats throughout your system won't help you, and may well harm you.

A NOTE ABOUT COMMON INGREDIENTS AND OVENS:

- When a recipe says 'eggs', we use extra-large (at least 59 g) eggs. Because dextrose sucks up any moisture, it's important to use bigger rather than smaller eggs.

- Vegetable oils (also known as polyunsaturated or seed oils) are dangerous to your health. All of the recipes in this book use olive oil or animal fats. For more, see my book *Big Fat Lies*.

- When a recipe says 'butter', we use unsalted butter. Dextrose has a mild sweetness which is overwhelmed by salted butter.

- When a recipe calls for buttermilk, you can buy it in the dairy section of your supermarket, but if you are only using a little and don't want to buy a whole carton, there are about 5 different ways of making it with ingredients you probably do have (including yoghurt and milk, lemon juice or white vinegar and milk, and sour cream and milk – just Google 'homemade buttermilk').

- Most of the oven temperatures in these recipes are altered from their sugar-based originals, but you may find that your oven does better if you reduce either the temperature or the baking time.

- Because dextrose has a lower burning point than sugar, it is a good idea to line cake tins and baking trays with a double layer of baking paper to prevent the outside burning before the centre of the cake or biscuit is cooked. Over-browning can also be minimised by using light-coloured rather than dark-coloured cake tins and trays, as dark bake-ware conducts more heat. If you find your cake or tart is browning very quickly, simply cover it loosely with a piece of baking paper for the remaining cooking time.

- As I've mentioned earlier, dextrose absorbs more liquid than sugar, so if you're worried that the texture of your batter or dough looks strange, then trust the recipe as it will work out in the end.

- -

WARNING! YOU CAN STILL GET FAT EATING DEXTROSE.

- -

You can force yourself to eat more than you need. If you get carried away with making some of these excellent recipes, you might find yourself with a constant supply of dextrose-based snacks. You will eat them, and then later you will eat a meal. You will struggle to finish the meal because you are full of yummy cake, but you might push through. If that becomes a regular habit, you will put on weight.

These recipes are for lunch-boxes, special occasions and for guests. You can have them without getting re-addicted or suffering any of the other ill effects of fructose consumption, but that does not mean you can stop listening to your appetite control system. If you eat half a cheesecake for afternoon tea, your appetite control will tell you not to eat again until (probably) lunchtime the next day. Listen to it or you will gain weight.

But don't let that put you off. You now hold in your hands the only comprehensive collection of non-addictive, non-artificially sweetened, restaurant-quality scrumalicious (yes I did make that up) sweet recipes ever gathered together between two covers – get cooking!

BREAD

KFAST

PANCAKES WITH MASCARPONE

MAKES 8

¾ cup self-raising flour, sifted

⅓ cup dextrose

2 eggs

¾ cup buttermilk

2 teaspoons vanilla essence,
   or to taste

butter, for pan-frying

mascarpone, blueberries (optional)
   and mint (optional), to serve

You can top these delicious fluffy pancakes with the strawberry jam on page 190 or rice malt syrup instead of blueberries and mascarpone, if you prefer.

1   Mix the flour and dextrose in a bowl. Make a well in the centre. Add the eggs, buttermilk and vanilla and whisk until smooth. Set aside for 10 minutes.

2   Heat a little butter in a large non-stick frying pan over medium heat. Cook a small ladleful (about 2 tablespoons) of the mixture for each pancake for 2–3 minutes on each side or until golden and cooked through.

3   Serve the pancakes immediately with mascarpone, blueberries and mint, if you like.

- - - - - - - - - - - - - - - - - - -

» VARIATION:

To make chocolate pancakes, replace ¼ cup of the flour with ¼ cup cocoa powder.

RICOTTA & CINNAMON MUFFINS

MAKES 12

2 cups plain flour

3 teaspoons ground cinnamon, or to taste

2 teaspoons baking powder

1¼ cups dextrose

1 cup firm ricotta, drained

2 eggs

½ cup milk

½ cup olive oil

1 tablespoon finely grated orange zest

2 teaspoons vanilla essence, or to taste

The addition of ricotta makes these moreish muffins light and moist.

1   Preheat the oven to 180°C (160°C fan-forced). Lightly grease and line a 12 hole-capacity muffin tin with paper cases.

2   Sift the flour, cinnamon and baking powder into a medium bowl. Add the dextrose and stir to combine.

3   In a separate bowl, whisk the ricotta, eggs, milk, oil, orange zest and vanilla until combined. Fold the ricotta mixture through the flour mixture until just combined; don't over-mix or the muffins will be tough. Spoon the batter evenly into the paper cases.

4   Bake the muffins for 30-35 minutes or until cooked when tested with a skewer. Leave to cool in the tin for 5 minutes, then transfer to a wire rack to cool.

5   Store any leftover muffins wrapped individually in plastic film or freezer bags in an airtight container in the freezer for up to 1 month.

- - - - - - - - - - - - - - - -

» VARIATION:

To vary the flavour of these muffins add fruit such as blueberries, mashed banana or unpeeled chopped or grated apple or pear.

GRANOLA BARS

MAKES 10

These are a terrific substitute for sugar-loaded purchased muesli bars.

2½ cups rolled oats
½ cup shredded coconut
½ cup pepitas (pumpkin seeds)
¼ cup sesame seeds
1 tablespoon ground cinnamon, or to taste
1 teaspoon vanilla essence, or to taste
1 cup glucose syrup
¼ cup dextrose
80 g unsalted butter, chopped

1 Preheat the oven to 170°C (150°C fan-forced). Grease and line a 30 cm × 20 cm slice tin with baking paper.

2 Mix the oats, coconut, pepitas, sesame seeds and cinnamon in a large bowl until well combined.

3 Put the vanilla, glucose, dextrose and butter into a small saucepan. Bring to the boil, then reduce the heat to medium and simmer for 2–3 minutes. Pour over the oat mixture and mix until well combined. Spoon into the prepared tin.

4 Bake the oat mixture for 25–30 minutes or until golden. Leave to cool completely in the tin.

5 Remove from the tin, then trim the edges and cut into ten 10 cm × 7 cm bars. Wrap each bar in baking paper. Store in an airtight container in the fridge for up to 2 days.

CRUNCHY GRANOLA WITH YOGHURT ❯

MAKES ABOUT 4 CUPS

You can add any nuts you like to this basic granola recipe – try walnuts, pecans, macadamias or almonds.

½ cup rice malt syrup
½ cup olive oil
3 cups rolled oats
½ cup sunflower seeds
½ cup pepitas (pumpkin seeds)
1 tablespoon ground cinnamon, or to taste
milk and natural yoghurt (such as Jalna Biodynamic yoghurt), to serve

1 Preheat the oven to 180°C (160°C fan-forced). Lightly grease a baking tray and line with baking paper.

2 Put the syrup and oil into a small saucepan and cook over low heat for 2 minutes, stirring until warmed through.

3 Mix the oats, sunflower seeds, pepitas and cinnamon in a bowl. Pour over the syrup mixture and stir to combine. Transfer the mixture to the prepared tray, spreading it out in an even layer.

4 Bake the granola for 20–25 minutes or until golden. Leave to cool on the tray. Serve with milk and yoghurt. Store in an airtight container for up to 7 days.

LEMON SCONES

MAKES 12

3 cups self-raising flour, sifted, plus extra for dusting

¾ cup dextrose

1 tablespoon finely grated lemon zest

75 g cold unsalted butter, chopped

1¼ cups buttermilk

milk, for brushing

Roasted Strawberry & Rhubarb Jam (see page 190) (optional), to serve

Enjoy these tangy scones for breakfast with strawberry jam or natural yoghurt, which can be mixed with a drop of vanilla essence for extra flavour. They are also a great addition to the school lunch-box or for an after-school treat.

1 Preheat the oven to 180°C (160°C fan-forced). Line a baking tray with baking paper.

2 Mix the flour, dextrose and lemon zest in a bowl to combine. Add the butter, then use your fingertips to rub it into the flour mixture until it resembles fine breadcrumbs. Make a well in the centre and pour in the buttermilk. Use a butter knife to gradually mix the buttermilk into the flour mixture until just combined.

3 Turn the dough out onto a lightly floured surface and gently bring it together. Roll out until 2 cm thick, then use a 6 cm round cutter to cut out 12 rounds. Put the scones onto the prepared tray and brush with milk.

4 Bake the scones for 18-20 minutes or until cooked when tested with a skewer.

5 Serve with strawberry jam, if you like. These are best eaten on the day they are made.

LITTLE COCONUT BREADS

MAKES 10

2 eggs

1⅓ cups coconut milk

2 teaspoons vanilla essence, or to taste

2¼ cups plain flour

2 teaspoons baking powder

1½ cups dextrose

1¼ cups desiccated coconut

75 g unsalted butter, melted

shredded coconut, for sprinkling

If you don't have mini loaf tins use a 21 cm × 9 cm loaf tin instead; just increase the cooking time to 45–50 minutes. You can then cut the loaf into slices, wrap them individually in plastic film and freeze until needed. I like these for breakfast, but they are also a welcome addition to school lunch-boxes or served for afternoon tea. Leftovers can be toasted and spread with butter.

1 Preheat the oven to 160°C (140°C fan-forced). Lightly grease and line ten ⅔ cup-capacity mini loaf tins.

2 Whisk the eggs, coconut milk and vanilla in a bowl.

3 Sift the flour and baking power into a large bowl. Add the dextrose and coconut and stir to combine. Make a well in the centre, then add the egg mixture and butter and stir to combine. Spoon the batter evenly into the prepared tins and sprinkle with shredded coconut.

4 Bake the breads for 25–30 minutes or until cooked when tested with a skewer. Leave to cool in the tins for 5 minutes, then turn out onto a wire rack to cool completely. Store any leftovers individually wrapped in plastic film or freezer bags in an airtight container in the freezer for up to 1 month.

SPICED PUMPKIN MUFFINS

MAKES 6

1½ cups plain flour
1 teaspoon baking powder
1 teaspoon ground cinnamon
1 teaspoon ground nutmeg
1 cup dextrose
1 cup cooled mashed pumpkin
⅓ cup olive oil
2 eggs

These lightly spiced muffins are a great way to use up leftover cooked pumpkin and taste a little bit like pumpkin pie. If you prefer the taste of wholemeal flour then use it instead of plain flour. Simply double the quantities if you wish to make 12 muffins.

1   Preheat the oven to 180°C (160°C fan forced). Lightly grease and line 6 holes of a 12 hole-capacity muffin tin with paper cases or baking paper.

2   Sift the flour, baking powder, cinnamon and nutmeg into a large bowl. Add the dextrose and stir to combine well.

3   Put the pumpkin, oil and eggs into a large bowl and whisk until smooth. Fold the pumpkin mixture into the flour mixture until just combined; don't over-mix or the muffins will be tough. Spoon the batter evenly into the prepared paper cases.

4   Bake the muffins for 30-35 minutes or until cooked when tested with a skewer. Transfer to a wire rack to cool.

5   Store any leftover muffins individually wrapped in plastic film or freezer bags in an airtight container in the freezer for up to 1 month.

» VARIATION:
Scatter the batter with pepitas (pumpkin seeds) before baking for a little extra crunch.

COOKI
BISC

ES &
UITS

DOUBLE CHOCOLATE CHIP COOKIES

MAKES 24

125 g unsalted butter, chopped
  and softened
1 cup dextrose
1 teaspoon vanilla essence,
  or to taste
1 egg
125 g plain flour, sifted
½ cup self-raising flour, sifted
40 g cocoa powder, sifted
½ teaspoon bicarbonate of soda
40 g Sugar-free Chocolate (see
  page 168), roughly chopped

To replicate an authentic chocolate chip experience, make your own chocolate chips with the sugar-free chocolate on page 168.

1 Preheat the oven to 170°C (150°C fan-forced). Line 2 baking trays with baking paper.

2 Beat the butter, dextrose and vanilla with an electric mixer until light and creamy. Add the egg and beat until just combined. Add the plain flour, self-raising flour, cocoa and bicarbonate of soda and continue to beat until just combined. Stir through the chopped chocolate.

3 Roll tablespoons of the dough into 24 balls and put onto the prepared trays, leaving room for them to spread a little, then flatten slightly.

4 Bake the cookies for 10-12 minutes or until cooked. Leave to cool on the trays for 5 minutes, then transfer to a wire rack to cool completely. Store in an airtight container for up to 2 days.

CLASSIC SHORTBREAD

MAKES 8 WEDGES

250 g cold unsalted
   butter, chopped
1½ cups dextrose, plus extra
   for dusting (optional)
1¼ cups plain flour, sifted
½ cup rice flour, sifted
2 teaspoons vanilla essence,
   or to taste

While shortbread can be made with plain flour alone,
adding rice flour produces a lighter result.

1 Preheat the oven to 170°C (150°C fan-forced). Lightly grease
   a 22 cm springform cake tin.

2 Process the butter, dextrose, plain flour, rice flour and vanilla
   in a food processor until the mixture just comes together to
   form a dough.

3 Lightly press the dough into the prepared tin, using the back
   of a spoon to smooth the top. Refrigerate for 15 minutes or
   until firm. Use a sharp knife to score the dough into 8 wedges
   and prick with a skewer.

4 Bake the shortbread for 40-50 minutes or until golden. Remove
   from the tin and leave to cool on a wire rack.

5 Cut into wedges and dust with extra dextrose, if desired, to serve.
   Store in an airtight container for up to 2 days.

- - - - - - - - - - - - - - - - - - -

» VARIATION:

If you wish to use this
shortbread recipe to make
individual biscuits, simply roll
out the dough until 5 mm or
so thick, then cut it into shapes
with your choice of cookie
cutter. It's the perfect base
recipe for making holiday-
themed cookies for Easter,
Christmas or Halloween.

ANZAC BISCUITS

MAKES 18

1 cup wholemeal plain flour, sifted
1 cup rolled oats
1 cup desiccated coconut
½ cup dextrose
125 g unsalted butter, chopped
⅓ cup rice malt syrup
1 tablespoon water
1 teaspoon bicarbonate of soda

Wholemeal flour adds a slight nutty taste to these traditional biscuits, but you can substitute it with plain flour if that's what's in your pantry. These are best eaten on the day they are made as they will soften a little when stored.

1   Preheat the oven to 160°C (140°C fan-forced). Line 2 baking trays with baking paper.

2   Mix the flour, oats, coconut and dextrose in a medium bowl.

3   Put the butter, syrup and water into a medium saucepan and bring just to the boil over medium heat. Whisk in the bicarbonate of soda and allow the mixture to foam up. Pour the butter mixture over the dry ingredients and stir until well combined.

4   Drop tablespoons of the mixture onto the prepared trays, leaving room between them for the mixture to spread.

5   Bake the biscuits for 20–25 minutes or until golden. Transfer to wire racks to cool completely. Store in an airtight container for up to 2 days.

- - - - - - - - - - - - - - - - - - - -

» VARIATION:

If you prefer a more cake-like texture, roll the mixture into balls, then only flatten them slightly before baking. For a crisper result, squash the dough flat before baking.

VANILLA STAR BISCUITS

MAKES 24

250 g unsalted butter, chopped
  and softened
1 cup dextrose
1 egg yolk
2 teaspoons vanilla essence,
  or to taste
2 cups plain flour, sifted

This is a terrific basic cookie dough to have in your repertoire. The kids can cut the dough into any shape they like, then decorate the finished biscuits with the egg-white icing on page 192.

1 Beat the butter and dextrose with an electric mixer for 8-10 minutes or until light and creamy. Add the egg yolk and vanilla and beat to combine. Add the flour and beat until a smooth dough forms.

2 Wrap the dough in plastic film and refrigerate for 30 minutes.

3 Preheat the oven to 180°C (160°C fan-forced). Line 2 baking trays with baking paper.

4 Roll out the dough between 2 sheets of baking paper until 5 mm thick. Use a 9 cm star-shaped cookie cutter to cut out cookies and place on the prepared baking trays.

5 Bake the biscuits for 10-12 minutes or until light golden. Leave to cool on the trays for 5 minutes, then transfer to wire racks to cool completely. Store in an airtight container for up to 2 days.

LEMON & PISTACHIO BISCOTTI

MAKES 24

3 egg whites
⅔ cup dextrose
½ cup plain flour, sifted
100 g peeled pistachios, chopped
2 tablespoons finely grated
   lemon zest

These biscotti are not as hard and crisp as sugar-based biscotti – they are a little softer and more bread-like. Perfect to have with a cup of tea.

1 Preheat the oven to 160°C (140°C fan-forced). Grease and line a 25 cm × 7 cm loaf tin.

2 Whisk the egg whites with an electric mixer until soft peaks form. With the motor running, gradually add the dextrose, whisking until stiff peaks form. Fold in the flour, pistachios and lemon zest until well combined. Spoon into the prepared loaf tin.

3 Bake the mixture for 35–40 minutes or until golden on top.

4 Remove from the tin, then leave on a wire rack to cool completely.

5 Increase the oven temperature to 180°C (160° fan-forced). Line 2 baking trays with baking paper.

6 Cut the biscotti into 1 cm-thick slices and put onto the prepared trays, cut-side down. Bake for 8–10 minutes or until just golden. Store in an airtight container for up to 2 days.

ORANGE & CHOCOLATE FLORENTINES

MAKES 46

2¾ cups dextrose
¼ cup glucose syrup
50 g unsalted butter, chopped
¼ cup thickened cream
100 g flaked almonds
2 tablespoons finely grated
   orange zest
⅓ cup plain flour, sifted
⅓ cup cocoa powder, sifted
½ cup boiling water

Florentines are traditionally made with candied cherries, however, we have used orange zest here instead. When combined with the chocolate glaze, the result is a delicious jaffa-like flavour.

1 Preheat the oven to 160°C (140° fan-forced). Line 2 baking trays with baking paper.

2 Put ¾ cup of the dextrose and the glucose, butter and cream into a medium saucepan and stir over medium heat until melted and combined. Bring to the boil, then reduce the heat to low and simmer for 6–9 minutes or until the mixture has thickened.

3 Remove the pan from the heat, then stir through the almonds, orange zest and flour. Place teaspoons of the mixture onto the prepared trays, leaving space between for them to spread.

4 Bake the biscuits for 5–7 minutes or until lacy and golden. Leave to cool completely on the trays.

5 Put the cocoa, water and remaining 2 cups dextrose into a medium heatproof bowl over a saucepan of boiling water and stir until melted and well combined; make sure the bottom of the bowl does not touch the water.

6 Dip half of each cooled biscuit into the chocolate mixture, then transfer to a baking tray lined with baking paper to cool and set. Store in an airtight container for up to 2 days.

CHOCOLATE CARAMEL SANDWICH BISCUITS

MAKES 16 SANDWICHES (32 BISCUITS)

150 g unsalted butter, chopped
and softened

⅔ cup dextrose

2 teaspoons vanilla essence,
or to taste

1¼ cups plain flour, sifted

2 tablespoons cocoa
powder, sifted

2 tablespoons cornflour, sifted

Caramel filling

1 cup dextrose

85 g unsalted butter, chopped

½ cup thickened cream

1 tablespoon cornflour

1 tablespoon water

The creamy caramel centre between these chocolate-y biscuits will win over any sugarholic. You can use the caramel as a filling for a caramel tart made with the pastry on page 80.

1 Beat the butter, dextrose and vanilla with an electric mixer for 8-10 minutes or until light and creamy. Add the flour, cocoa and cornflour and beat until a dough forms. Form the dough into a disc, then wrap in plastic film and refrigerate for 30 minutes.

2 Preheat the oven to 180°C (160°C fan-forced). Line 2 baking trays with baking paper.

3 Roll out the dough between 2 sheets of baking paper until 5 mm thick. Use a 5 cm cookie cutter to cut out rounds from the dough, placing them on the prepared trays as you go.

4 Bake the biscuits for 10-12 minutes or until just dry and cooked. Cool on the trays for 5 minutes, then transfer to wire racks to cool completely.

5 To make the caramel filling, whisk the dextrose in a saucepan over high heat until melted. Bring to the boil and cook for 2-3 minutes or until golden. Carefully whisk in the butter, then remove from the heat and whisk in the cream. Put the cornflour and water into a small jug and whisk until smooth, then add to the pan. Return the pan to low heat, then stir the mixture continuously for 3-4 minutes or until thickened. Leave to cool completely.

6 Spread the caramel filling over half of the cooled biscuits and sandwich with the remaining biscuits. Store in an airtight container for up to 2 days.

PISTACHIO & ALMOND BISCUITS

MAKES ABOUT 24

125 g unsalted butter, chopped
    and softened

½ cup dextrose

1 egg, lightly beaten

1 teaspoon vanilla essence,
    or to taste

2 tablespoons natural yoghurt
    (I use Jalna Biodynamic yoghurt)

1 cup rice flour

½ cup blanched almonds, chopped

¼ cup peeled pistachios, chopped

¼ cup sunflower seeds

These crunchy biscuits are also gluten-free, making them the ideal choice if you're cooking for someone with a gluten intolerance.

1 Preheat the oven to 180°C (160°C fan-forced). Line 2 baking trays with baking paper.

2 Beat the butter and dextrose with an electric mixer until light and creamy. Add the egg and vanilla and beat to combine. Fold in the yoghurt, rice flour, nuts and sunflower seeds.

3 Roll tablespoons of the mixture into balls and put onto the prepared trays, then flatten slightly with a fork.

4 Bake the biscuits for 10-12 minutes or until light golden. Cool on the trays for 5 minutes, then transfer to a wire rack to cool completely. Store in an airtight container for up to 3 days.

COCONUT MACAROONS

MAKES 18

3 egg whites
½ cup dextrose
3 cups shredded coconut
¼ cup plain flour, sifted
1 teaspoon vanilla essence,
   or to taste

If you prefer the softer, white and chewy result that using untoasted coconut offers use this instead. Alternatively, you can toast the coconut before mixing it in with the egg and flour, if you favour a crisp and crunchy result.

1 Preheat the oven to 180°C (160°C fan-forced). Line 2 baking trays with baking paper.

2 Whisk the egg whites with an electric mixer until soft peaks form. With the motor running, gradually add the dextrose, whisking until stiff peaks form. Fold in the coconut, flour and vanilla until well combined. Spoon tablespoons of the mixture onto the prepared trays.

3 Bake the macaroons for 15-20 minutes or until golden. Leave to cool on the trays. Store in an airtight container for up to 3 days.

PEANUT BISCUITS

MAKES 12

½ cup self-raising flour, sifted
½ cup plain flour, sifted
½ cup dextrose
125 g peanuts, toasted and
  roughly chopped
1 egg, lightly beaten
100 g unsalted butter, chopped
  and softened
1 teaspoon sea salt

These salty, nutty biscuits satisfy cravings for peanut cookies usually made with sugar laden store-bought peanut butter.

1 Preheat the oven to 180°C (160°C fan-forced). Line a baking tray with baking paper.

2 Put the self-raising flour, plain flour, dextrose and peanuts into a bowl. Add the egg and butter and mix until well combined.

3 Roll tablespoons of the mixture into balls, then put onto the prepared tray, leaving room between them for the mixture to spread. Press gently to flatten. Sprinkle with the salt.

4 Bake the biscuits for 15-20 minutes or until golden. Cool on the tray for 5 minutes, then transfer to a wire rack to cool completely. Store in an airtight container for up to 2 days.

COFFEE & CHOCOLATE BUTTERCREAM SANDWICHES

MAKES 16 SANDWICHES (32 BISCUITS)

185 g unsalted butter, chopped
  and softened
1 cup dextrose, plus extra
  for dusting
1 teaspoon vanilla essence,
  or to taste
1 egg yolk, lightly beaten
1 tablespoon milk
¼ cup strong coffee
3 cups plain flour, sifted

Chocolate buttercream
150 g unsalted butter, chopped
½ cup dextrose
2 tablespoons milk
2 tablespoons cocoa powder, sifted
2 teaspoons vanilla essence,
  or to taste

The coffee shortbreads can be eaten alone or sandwiched with the buttercream for a more indulgent treat.

1   Beat the butter, dextrose and vanilla with an electric mixer until light and creamy. Add the egg yolk, milk and coffee and beat until well combined. Add the flour and beat until just combined. Form the dough into a disc, then wrap in plastic film and refrigerate for 30 minutes.

2   Preheat the oven to 180°C (160°C fan-forced). Line 2 baking trays with baking paper.

3   Roll out the dough between 2 sheets of baking paper until 5 mm thick. Use a 5 cm fluted cookie cutter to cut out rounds from the dough. Put onto the prepared baking trays, leaving room between for them to spread.

4   Bake the biscuits for 10–12 minutes or until just golden and cooked. Cool on the trays for 5 minutes, then transfer to wire racks to cool completely.

5   To make the buttercream, beat the butter, dextrose, milk, cocoa and vanilla with an electric mixer until light and creamy.

6   Spread the buttercream over half of the biscuits and sandwich with the remaining biscuits. Dust with extra dextrose, if you like. Store in an airtight container for up to 4 days.

CUPC
&C
&

AKES
AKES

VANILLA CUPCAKES

MAKES 12

120 g unsalted butter, chopped
and softened

1 cup dextrose

2 teaspoons vanilla essence,
or to taste

2 eggs

2 cups self-raising flour, sifted

1 cup milk

Italian meringue icing

50 g unsalted butter, softened

¾ cup dextrose

1 tablespoon water

2 egg whites

pinch of cream of tartar

- - - - - - - - - - - - - - - - -

» VARIATION :

To make one large vanilla cake,
lightly grease and line a 20 cm
cake tin with baking paper,
then add the batter. Bake for
35-40 minutes or until cooked
when tested with a skewer.

The icing on these cupcakes has been caramelised with
a kitchen blowtorch – you could replicate this effect by
placing the iced cakes under a hot griller or leave as is.
Alternatively, ice the cakes with the icing on page 192.

1   Preheat the oven to 180°C (160°C fan-forced). Line a 12 ½ cup-
capacity hole muffin tin with paper cases.

2   Beat the butter, dextrose and vanilla with an electric mixer until
light and creamy. With the motor running, add the eggs, beating
until well combined. Alternately fold in the flour and milk until
the batter is smooth. Spoon into the prepared cases.

3   Bake the cakes for 15-20 minutes or until cooked when tested
with a skewer. Transfer to a wire rack to cool completely.

4   To make the icing, beat the butter with the electric mixer until
light and creamy. Transfer to a clean bowl and set aside. Put
the dextrose and water into a small saucepan and bring to the
boil over medium heat, then cook until the syrup reaches soft
ball stage (121°C on a candy thermometer). To test, place a drop
of hot syrup in a cup of cold water - it should easily form a ball
when rolled between 2 fingers. Whisk the egg whites and cream
of tartar with the clean, dry electric mixer until soft peaks form.
With the motor running, gradually pour in the dextrose syrup,
continuing to whisk until the mixture is thick, glossy and cold.
Add the butter and whisk until well combined.

5   Spread the icing on the cooled cupcakes and eat on the day
they are made. Store uniced cakes in an airtight container in
the freezer for up to 1 month.

MACADAMIA BROWNIES

SERVES 8-10

2 cups dextrose

4 eggs

250 g unsalted butter, melted and cooled

1¼ cups plain flour, sifted

½ cup cocoa powder, sifted, plus extra for dusting

½ teaspoon baking powder, sifted

100 g macadamias, toasted and roughly chopped

A brownie should still be soft in the centre so take care not to overcook; it will set as it cools. These brownies are on the cake-y rather than fudgy side.

1 Preheat the oven to 180°C (160°C fan-forced). Grease and line a 22 cm square cake tin with baking paper.

2 Put the dextrose and eggs into a medium bowl and whisk until light and creamy. Add the melted butter, flour, cocoa and baking powder and stir to combine. Fold in the macadamias. Pour the batter into the prepared tin.

3 Bake for 35 minutes or until cooked but still soft in the centre. Leave to cool completely in the tin. Cut into squares, then dust with cocoa and serve. Store in an airtight container for up to 3 days.

- - - - - - - - - - - - - - - - - -

» VARIATION :

The addition of macadamias give these brownies the extra crunch you would usually get from chocolate bits, but you can leave them out, or use other nuts such as almonds or walnuts, if you prefer.

SPONGE CAKE WITH JAM & CREAM

SERVES 8

225 g unsalted butter, chopped
 and softened

1 cup dextrose, plus extra
 for dusting

1 teaspoon vanilla essence,
 or to taste

4 eggs

1⅓ cups self-raising flour, sifted

25 g cornflour, sifted

¼ cup milk

1 cup Roasted Strawberry &
 Rhubarb Jam (see page 190)

1 cup thickened cream, whipped

- - - - - - - - - - - - - - - - -

» VARIATION:

This sponge is equally delicious
spread with the passionfruit or
lemon curd on page 193 instead
of jam.

We all need a fail-safe sponge recipe in our repertoire and
this one fits the bill. While not quite as feather-light as
the classic version, it is deliciously moist when filled with
whipped cream and jam.

1 Preheat the oven to 180°C (160°C fan-forced). Grease and
 line two 20 cm springform cake tins with baking paper.

2 Beat the butter, dextrose and vanilla with an electric mixer
 until light and creamy. Add one egg at a time, beating well
 after adding each one. Fold in the flour and cornflour until
 well combined. Fold in the milk. Spoon the batter evenly
 into the prepared tins.

3 Bake the cakes for 20-25 minutes or until they come away
 from the edge of the tins. Leave the cakes to cool in the tins
 for 10 minutes, then turn out onto wire racks to cool completely.

4 Spread one cake with jam and cream, then top with the other
 cake and dust with extra dextrose. This cake is best eaten on
 the day it is made.

RED VELVET FAIRY CAKES

MAKES 12

200 g unsalted butter, chopped and softened

2 cups dextrose, plus extra for dusting

1 teaspoon vanilla essence, or to taste

3 eggs

2 cups plain flour

¼ cup cocoa powder

1 teaspoon bicarbonate of soda

1 cup buttermilk

red food colouring, as needed

1 cup thickened cream, whipped

- -

» VARIATION:

To make two large cakes, use 2 cups self-raising flour instead of the plain flour. Pour the batter into two greased and lined 20 cm cake tins and bake for 35–40 minutes or until cooked when tested with a skewer.

You could ice the uncut tops of these tempting little cakes with the chocolate glaze on page 92 instead of filling them with whipped cream, if preferred.

1   Preheat the oven to 180°C (160°C fan-forced). Line a 12 hole-capacity muffin tin with paper cases.

2   Beat the butter, dextrose and vanilla with an electric mixer until light and creamy. Add one egg at a time, beating well after adding each one.

3   Sift the flour, cocoa and bicarbonate of soda into a medium bowl and whisk until well combined. With the motor running, alternately add the flour mixture and buttermilk to the butter mixture and beat until just combined. Fold in the food colouring until the batter is your desired colour. Spoon evenly into the prepared paper cases.

4   Bake the cakes for 25–30 minutes or until cooked when tested with a skewer. Cool in the tin for 5 minutes, then transfer to a wire rack to cool completely.

5   Use a teaspoon to carefully scoop out the centre of each cupcake (see photo), reserving the tops. Spoon a tablespoon of whipped cream into each hole, then top with the reserved cake tops. (You can cut the reserved cake tops in half, then position them in the cream to resemble fairy wings, if you like.) Dust with extra dextrose. These cakes are best eaten on the day they are made. Store any leftover cakes wrapped in plastic film or freezer bags in an airtight container in the freezer for up to 1 month.

ALMOND TEA CAKE

SERVES 8-10

225 g unsalted butter, chopped and softened

1 cup dextrose, plus extra for dusting

1 teaspoon vanilla essence, or to taste

2 tablespoons finely grated lemon zest

3 eggs

1 cup self-raising flour, sifted

1 teaspoon baking powder, sifted

2 cups ground almonds

½ cup milk

whipped cream (optional), to serve

Serve this rich buttery cake with cream and raspberries for a special occasion or as is for afternoon tea – or just with cream…

1 Preheat the oven to 170°C (150°C fan-forced). Lightly grease a 22 cm round cake tin and line it with 2 layers of baking paper (this helps to prevent the edges from burning).

2 Beat the butter, dextrose, vanilla and lemon zest with an electric mixer until light and creamy. Add one egg at a time, beating well after adding each one. Add the flour, baking powder, ground almonds and milk and beat until well combined. Spoon the batter into the prepared tin.

3 Bake the cake for 30-35 minutes or until cooked when tested with a skewer. Leave to cool in the tin for 5 minutes, then turn out onto a wire rack to cool completely. Dust with extra dextrose to serve. Store in an airtight container in the fridge for up to 3 days.

ORANGE POLENTA CAKE

SERVES 8-10

185 g unsalted butter, chopped and softened

1 cup dextrose

1 tablespoon finely grated orange zest

1 teaspoon vanilla essence, or to taste

3 eggs

1½ cups self-raising flour, sifted

1 cup polenta

¾ cup milk

double cream (optional), to serve

Orange glaze

1 cup water

1 cup dextrose

zest of 1 orange, removed with a vegetable peeler

The addition of polenta gives this orange-scented cake a wonderful, almost crunchy texture.

1 Preheat the oven to 180°C (160°C fan-forced). Grease and line a 22 cm ring cake tin with 2 layers of baking paper.

2 Beat the butter, dextrose, orange zest and vanilla with an electric mixer until light and creamy. Add one egg at a time, beating well after adding each one. Add the flour, polenta and milk and continue to beat until smooth and well combined. Spoon the batter into the prepared tin.

3 Bake the cake for 35-40 minutes or until cooked when tested with a skewer.

4 Meanwhile, to make the orange glaze, put the water, dextrose and orange zest into a small saucepan and bring to the boil over high heat. Simmer for 8-10 minutes or until thickened. Pour over the warm cake in the tin and leave to cool completely.

5 Serve the cake with double cream, if desired. Store in an airtight container for up to 2 days. Leftover slices of cake may be individually wrapped in plastic film or freezer bags and stored in an airtight container in the freezer for up to 1 month.

CINNAMON TEA CAKE

SERVES 8-10

200 g unsalted butter, chopped
and softened

1½ cups dextrose

2 teaspoons vanilla essence,
or to taste

3 eggs

1½ cups plain flour, sifted

1 teaspoon baking powder, sifted

1½ teaspoons ground cinnamon

½ cup sour cream

Cinnamon topping

1½ tablespoons dextrose

1 teaspoon ground cinnamon

50 g unsalted butter, melted

This favourite Australian cake is sure to bring a smile
to anyone's face when it appears on the table.

1 Preheat the oven to 160°C (140°C fan-forced). Grease and line
a 22 cm springform cake tin with 2 layers of baking paper.

2 Beat the butter, dextrose and vanilla with an electric mixer
until light and creamy. Add one egg at a time, beating well
after adding each one. Fold in the flour, baking powder,
cinnamon and sour cream. Spoon the batter into the
prepared tin.

3 Bake the cake for 1 hour or until it is cooked when tested
with a skewer. Cool in the tin for 5 minutes, then turn out
onto a wire rack to cool completely.

4 To make the topping, combine the dextrose and cinnamon.
Brush the warm cake with melted butter, then sprinkle over
the cinnamon mixture and serve. Store leftover slices of the
cake individually wrapped in plastic film or freezer bags in
an airtight container in the freezer for up to 1 month.

LEMON FRIANDS

MAKES 12

5 egg whites

1¼ cups ground almonds

1⅓ cups dextrose, plus extra
for dusting

½ cup plain flour, sifted

2 tablespoons finely grated
lemon zest

190 g unsalted butter, melted

The addition of ground almonds makes friands lighter than their muffin cousins. Just be sure to grease your friand tin well. If the tin is no longer shiny and new you may want to lightly dust it with flour as well as this helps stop the batter from sticking.

1   Preheat the oven to 180°C (160°C fan-forced). Lightly grease a 12-hole friand tin or 12 friand moulds.

2   Whisk the egg whites with an electric mixer until soft peaks form.

3   Mix the ground almonds, dextrose, flour and lemon zest in a medium bowl. Fold in the butter and egg whites until well combined. Spoon evenly into the prepared tin/moulds.

4   Bake the friands for 25–30 minutes or until cooked when tested with a skewer. Cool in the tin/moulds for 5 minutes, then turn out onto a wire rack to cool completely. Dust with extra dextrose before serving. Store leftovers individually wrapped in plastic film or freezer bags in an airtight container in the freezer for up to 1 month.

- - - - - - - - - - - - - - - - - - -

» VARIATIONS:

Try replacing the lemon zest with orange zest or fold through some whole raspberries before baking.

LEMON CAKES WITH EARL GREY ICING

MAKES 4

125 g unsalted butter, chopped
and softened

1 cup dextrose

2 tablespoons finely grated
lemon zest

2 eggs

1¼ cups self-raising flour, sifted

⅓ cup milk

Earl grey icing

2 earl grey teabags

⅓ cup boiling water

1 cup dextrose

¼ teaspoon cream of tartar

2 egg whites

Lemon syrup

1 cup dextrose

½ cup water

zest of 1 lemon, removed in long,
thin strips with a citrus zester

- - - - - - - - - - - - - - - - -

» VARIATIONS:

To make a large cake, grease
and line a 20 cm square cake
tin with baking paper. Add
the batter and bake for 30-35
minutes or until cooked when
tested with a skewer. The cake is
also delicious without the icing,
or use chai tea bags instead.

These pretty little cakes are the perfect treat for high tea.
Double the quantities to make eight cakes, if you like.

1   Preheat the oven to 180°C (160°C fan-forced). Grease and line
four 1 cup-capacity mini bundt tins or texas muffin tin holes.

2   Beat the butter, dextrose and lemon zest with an electric mixer
until light and creamy. Add one egg at a time, beating well after
adding each one. Alternately fold in the flour and milk and spoon
evenly into the prepared tins. Bake the cakes for 25-30 minutes
or until cooked when tested with a skewer. Leave to cool in the
tin for 5 minutes, then transfer to a wire rack to cool completely.

3   For the icing, put the teabags and boiling water into a small
saucepan and stand for 5-10 minutes. Remove the teabags and
discard. Add the dextrose and cream of tartar to the pan
and bring to the boil over medium heat, then continue to
boil until the liquid reaches soft ball stage (121°C on a candy
thermometer). To test, place a drop of hot syrup in a cup of cold
water - it should easily form a ball when rolled between 2 fingers.
Whisk the egg whites with the clean and dry electric mixer until
soft peaks form. With the motor running, gradually pour in the
dextrose syrup, whisking for 5-6 minutes or until thick and
glossy. Spread the icing on the cooled cakes.

4   For the lemon syrup, put the dextrose, water and lemon zest into
a small saucepan, then bring to the boil over high heat. Simmer
for 8-10 minutes or until the syrup is thick and glossy. Immediately
spoon the lemon syrup over the iced cakes and serve.

CHOCOLATE FUDGE CAKE WITH CHOCOLATE ICING

SERVES 8-10

200 g unsalted butter, chopped
   and softened

1 cup dextrose

1 teaspoon vanilla essence,
   or to taste

2 eggs

¾ cup buttermilk

1⅓ cups plain flour, sifted

⅓ cup cocoa powder, sifted

1 teaspoon bicarbonate
   of soda, sifted

Chocolate icing

3 cups dextrose, plus extra
   if needed

1 cup cocoa powder, sifted

200 g unsalted butter, chopped
   and softened

¾ cup milk, plus extra if needed

1 tablespoon vanilla essence,
   or to taste

This is a great celebration cake, perfect for birthday parties, and will be a family favourite with this fudgy chocolate icing.

1 Preheat the oven to 180°C (160°C fan-forced). Grease and line a 20 cm round cake tin with 2 layers of baking paper.

2 Beat the butter, dextrose and vanilla with an electric mixer until light and creamy. Add one egg at a time, beating well after adding each one. Alternately fold in the buttermilk, flour, cocoa and bicarbonate of soda until well combined. Spoon the batter into the prepared tin.

3 Bake the cake for 45-50 minutes or until cooked when tested with a skewer. Cool in the tin for 5 minutes, then turn out onto a wire rack and leave to cool completely.

4 To make the icing, combine the dextrose and cocoa in a small bowl. Beat the butter with the electric mixer for 2 minutes or until light and creamy. Add the milk, vanilla and half of the dextrose mixture. Continue to beat for 3-5 minutes, then add the remaining dextrose mixture and beat for a further 3-5 minutes or until the mixture is light and fluffy. (If the icing is too dry, add a little more milk. If it is too wet, add a little extra dextrose.)

5 Spread the icing over the cooled cake, then serve. Store leftover slices wrapped in plastic film or freezer bags in an airtight container in the freezer for up to 2 weeks.

STICKY CARAMEL BUNDT CAKE

SERVES 8-10

250 g unsalted butter, melted

1½ cups dextrose

1 teaspoon vanilla essence, or to taste

4 eggs

2½ cups plain flour, sifted, plus extra for dusting

1½ teaspoons baking powder, sifted

1 cup milk

thickened or double cream (optional), to serve

Caramel sauce

1 cup dextrose

85 g unsalted butter, chopped

½ cup thickened cream

1 tablespoon cornflour

1 tablespoon water

This delicious caramel cake doubles as a perfect pudding to offer visitors. Serve it warm with the hot caramel sauce and cream and enjoy the accolades of your happy guests.

1 Preheat the oven to 180°C (160°C fan-forced). Grease a 1.5 litre-capacity bundt tin and dust with flour.

2 Beat the butter, dextrose and vanilla with an electric mixer for 8-10 minutes or until light and creamy. Add one egg at a time, beating well after adding each one. Add the flour, baking powder and milk and beat until well combined. Spoon the mixture into the prepared tin.

3 Bake the cake for 35-40 minutes or until cooked when tested with a skewer. Leave the cake to cool in the tin for 5 minutes, then turn out onto a wire rack and leave to cool while you make the caramel sauce.

4 To make the caramel sauce, put the dextrose into a small saucepan and whisk over high heat until it has melted. Bring to the boil and cook for 2-3 minutes or until golden. Carefully whisk in the butter until well combined. Remove from the heat and stir in the cream. Put the cornflour and water into a small jug and whisk until smooth. Add to the saucepan and stir to combine, then bring to the boil over high heat. Cool slightly, then pour over the warm cake.

5 Serve the cake with cream, if desired. This cake is best eaten on the day it is made. Store leftover slices individually wrapped in plastic film or freezer bags in an airtight container in the freezer for up to 1 month.

CHOCOLATE MOUSSE CAKE

SERVES 8

225 g unsalted butter

¾ cup cocoa powder, sifted, plus
extra for dusting (optional)

5 eggs

2 cups dextrose

2 teaspoons vanilla essence,
or to taste

This simple, light flourless cake is the perfect choice for dessert when entertaining. Make it the day before and store it in the fridge, then remove from the fridge an hour or so before serving to bring it back to room temperature.

1 Preheat the oven to 180°C (160°C fan-forced). Grease and line a 22 cm springform cake tin with 2 layers of baking paper.

2 Put the butter and cocoa into a medium saucepan, then stir over medium heat until melted and smooth. Set aside.

3 Whisk the eggs, dextrose and vanilla with an electric mixer for 8–10 minutes or until doubled in size and thickened with a mousse-like texture. Fold through the butter mixture and pour into the prepared tin.

4 Bake the cake for 50–60 minutes or until just set (the cake will be soft and gooey in the middle, rather like a fondant).

5 Refrigerate overnight before serving. Bring to room temperature, then dust with cocoa powder, if desired, and serve.

- - - - - - - - - - - - - - - - - - - -

» VARIATION:

For a choc-mint flavoured cake, use a few drops of natural peppermint essence instead of vanilla essence.

TARTS,
TORT
&

TES
PIES

APPLE TARTE TATIN

SERVES 6-8

plain flour, for dusting
1 × 375 g block butter puff pastry
1 cup dextrose
50 g unsalted butter, chopped
4 pink lady apples, cored and
  cut into 8 wedges each
double cream or Custard
  (see page 192), to serve

You can use whatever size heavy-based ovenproof frying pan you have to make this classic French upside-down tart. Just be sure to cut the pastry round 2 cm bigger than the diameter of your pan so there's enough pastry to tuck in the edges and cover the fruit.

1 Preheat the oven to 200°C (180°C fan-forced).

2 Lightly dust a bench-top with flour, then roll out the pastry until 5 mm thick. Use a dinner plate as a guide to cut out a pastry round, then set aside.

3 Heat the dextrose in a 22 cm ovenproof non-stick frying pan over high heat, whisking until melted. Bring to the boil and continue to cook without stirring or touching until it turns a caramel colour. Carefully whisk in the butter. Immediately remove the pan from the heat and arrange the apple wedges on top.

4 Put the pastry over the apple, folding the edges under at the sides and tucking the apple in. Use a small sharp knife to make 3 small cuts in the centre of the pastry to allow steam to escape. Put the pan onto a baking tray to catch any overflowing juices.

5 Bake the tart for 25-30 minutes or until the pastry is puffed and golden. Leave to stand in the pan for 5 minutes, then turn out onto a plate. Serve with cream or custard.

» VARIATION:

While it's traditional to use apples in tarte tatin, you could use another firm fruit such as pears or plums instead.

CHOCOLATE TORTE WITH COFFEE MASCARPONE

SERVES 6-8

110 g unsalted butter, chopped and softened

2 cups dextrose

2 teaspoons vanilla essence, or to taste

4 eggs

2 cups self-raising flour, sifted

½ cup cocoa powder, sifted, plus extra for dusting

1 cup milk

Coffee mascarpone

1 tablespoon instant coffee

1 tablespoon boiling water

250 g mascarpone

½ cup dextrose

- - - - - - - - - - - - - - - - - - - -

» VARIATION:

As this recipe makes 2 cakes you could halve the quantities to make a single chocolate cake (or make both cakes and freeze one for another time). Simply ice the cake with the chocolate icing on page 64 or the chocolate fudge icing on page 172.

If you are lucky enough to have any of this luscious cake left over, briefly heat slices in the microwave and serve them with the chocolate fudge sauce on page 191 and ice cream on page 124 for a wonderful dessert!

1   Preheat the oven to 180°C (160°C fan-forced). Grease and line two 20 cm round cake tins with 2 layers of baking paper.

2   Beat the butter, dextrose and vanilla with an electric mixer until light and creamy. Add one egg at a time, beating well after adding each one.

3   Add the flour, cocoa and milk and beat until the mixture is smooth and well combined. Spoon half of the batter into each of the prepared cake tins.

4   Bake the cakes for 50-60 minutes or until cooked when tested with a skewer. Turn out onto wire racks to cool completely.

5   Meanwhile, to make the coffee mascarpone, put the coffee and water into a small jug or bowl and stir until the coffee has dissolved. Put the mascarpone into a medium bowl and whisk until softened. Add the dextrose and the coffee mixture and mix until well combined.

6   Spread half of the mascarpone mixture onto one of the cooled cakes and top with the remaining cake and mascarpone. Dust with extra cocoa. This is best eaten on the day it is made. Store leftover slices of cake wrapped in plastic film or freezer bags in an airtight container in the freezer for up to 2 weeks.

RHUBARB COBBLERS

SERVES 6

500 g rhubarb stalks, chopped
2 cups dextrose
2 star anise
1 cinnamon stick

Cobbler topping
1 cup self-raising flour, sifted
¼ cup dextrose
1 teaspoon vanilla essence,
  or to taste
75 g cold unsalted butter, chopped
¼ cup milk

Here is a quick alternative to a pastry-enclosed pie.
If you're not keen on rhubarb then you can use the
cobbler topping to cover any stewed fruit. Try serving
this with the caramel sauce on page 67 or custard on
page 192 – or both if you like!

1 Preheat the oven to 180°C (160°C fan-forced).

2 Put the rhubarb, dextrose, star anise and cinnamon into a medium
   saucepan. Cook over medium heat, stirring for 5 minutes or until
   the dextrose has dissolved and the rhubarb has softened slightly.
   Remove and discard the cinnamon and star anise. Divide the
   rhubarb among six 1½ cup-capacity ramekins. Set aside.

3 To make the cobbler topping, mix the flour, dextrose and
   vanilla in a large bowl. Add the butter and, using your
   fingertips, rub it into the flour mixture until the mixture
   resembles fine breadcrumbs. Gradually add the milk, stirring
   until a dough forms. Divide the dough into 6 rounds to fit
   the tops of the ramekins. Place one on top of the rhubarb
   mixture in each ramekin.

4 Bake the cobblers for 30 minutes or until the topping is
   golden and cooked when tested with a skewer. Serve.

PASSIONFRUIT TARTLETS

MAKES 4

olive oil spray, for greasing
1 quantity Passionfruit Curd
  (see page 193)

Coconut pastry
1 cup plain flour
1 cup shredded coconut
¼ cup dextrose
90 g cold unsalted butter, chopped
1 egg yolk

The tropical touch of coconut in the pastry is a perfect match for the slight tang of the passionfruit curd filling. These tarts can be prepared in advance and refrigerated; just remove them from the fridge to return to room temperature for one to two hours before serving to make the passionfruit curd nice and soft.

1 To make the pastry, process the flour, coconut, dextrose, butter and egg yolk in a food processor until the mixture just comes together to form a dough. Gently press the dough into a disc, then wrap in plastic film and refrigerate for 30 minutes.

2 Preheat the oven to 180°C (160°C fan-forced). Spray four 9 cm tart tins with removable bases with olive oil spray.

3 Divide the dough into quarters, then roll out each piece until 5 mm thick and use to line the prepared tins. Prick the bases with a fork. Bake for 10-12 minutes or until crisp and golden. Leave to cool completely.

4 Spoon the passionfruit curd into the tartlet shells and serve.

» VARIATIONS:

For little lemon tarts, simply replace the passionfruit curd with the lemon curd on page 193. If you prefer to make one large tart, use a 21 cm flan tin instead of individual tins and bake for 20-25 minutes or until golden.

PECAN PIE

SERVES 6

¾ cup dextrose
½ cup glucose syrup
40 g unsalted butter
3 eggs
¼ cup thickened cream
2 teaspoons vanilla essence,
   or to taste
125 g pecan halves
thickened cream,
   to serve (optional)

Sweet pastry
1⅔ cups plain flour, sifted
2 tablespoons dextrose
¼ teaspoon baking powder, sifted
180 g cold unsalted butter, chopped
¼–⅓ cup iced water
1½ teaspoons vanilla essence,
   or to taste

- - - - - - - - - - - - - - - - - -

》 VARIATION:
You can also use the pastry
and filling to make individual
muffin-sized pecan pies using
a greased muffin tin. Bake for
25-30 minutes or until golden
and set.

Universally loved by sugar addicts and those who have
kicked the sugar habit, this is the perfect contribution
to the dessert table at your next celebration. If the filling
starts to become too dark, simply cover it with foil for the
remainder of the cooking time.

1 To make the pastry, process the flour, dextrose and baking
   powder in a food processor until combined. Add the butter and
   process until the mixture resembles fine breadcrumbs. With the
   motor running, gradually add the water and vanilla and process
   until the mixture comes together to form a smooth dough.
   Shape into a disc, then wrap in plastic film and refrigerate
   for 30 minutes.

2 Lightly grease a 34 cm × 11 cm rectangular tart tin. Roll the
   pastry out between 2 sheets of baking paper until 3 mm thick.
   Line the prepared tin with the pastry. Trim the edges using
   a small, sharp knife. Refrigerate for 30 minutes.

3 Preheat the oven to 170°C (150°C fan-forced).

4 Put the dextrose, glucose syrup and butter into a saucepan and
   stir over low heat for 2-3 minutes or until melted and combined.
   Transfer to a bowl, then add the eggs, cream and vanilla and
   whisk to combine. Pour into the tin and top with the pecans.
   Place the tin on a baking tray.

5 Bake the tart for 1 hour or until golden and set. Cool completely.
   Serve with cream, if desired. Store in an airtight container in the
   fridge for up to 2 days.

APPLE & RHUBARB PIE

SERVES 8-10

10 granny smith apples, cored and roughly chopped

2 cups dextrose

2 teaspoons ground cinnamon

500 g rhubarb stalks, roughly chopped

1 quantity Sweet Pastry (see page 80)

1 cup ground almonds

1 egg, beaten

Just the thing to cheer up your loved ones on a cold winter's night, this old-fashioned favourite is perfect served with the custard on page 192 alongside.

1 Put the apple, dextrose and cinnamon into a large saucepan. Cook over medium heat, stirring for 10-12 minutes. Add the rhubarb and cook for a further 5 minutes or until the fruit has softened but the apple still holds its shape. Leave to cool completely.

2 Preheat the oven to 200°C (180°C fan-forced). Lightly grease a 20 cm pie tin or dish.

3 Roll two-thirds of the pastry out between 2 sheets of baking paper until 3 mm thick and use to line the pie dish. Roll the remaining pastry to make a 22 cm round for the pie lid.

4 Scatter the ground almonds over the base of the pastry, then spoon over the apple and rhubarb filling. Top with the pie lid, trimming the edges with a small, sharp knife. Use a fork to seal the edges. Cut a small slit in the centre to allow steam to escape. Brush the lid with the beaten egg.

5 Bake the pie for 30-35 minutes or until the pastry is golden and cooked through. Serve warm.

» VARIATION:

If you are short of time, use 2 sheets of store-bought butter puff pastry instead of making your own.

CHILLED VANILLA CHEESECAKE

SERVES 6-8

500 g cream cheese, chopped

2 tablespoons finely grated lemon zest

2 teaspoons vanilla essence, or to taste

1½ cups dextrose

2 cups thickened cream

Coconut base

¾ cup plain flour, sifted

⅓ cup desiccated coconut

⅓ cup dextrose

100 g unsalted butter, melted

This vanilla and lemon-scented cheesecake is everything a chilled cheesecake should be – soft, creamy and absolutely luscious. The set of this version is not as firm as a baked one, so it is best eaten straight from the fridge.

1   Preheat the oven to 170°C (150°C fan-forced). Lightly grease a 22 cm springform cake tin and line with baking paper.

2   To make the base, mix the flour, coconut, dextrose and butter in a bowl until combined. Press into the base of the prepared tin.

3   Bake the base for 20-25 minutes or until golden. Leave to cool completely.

4   Beat the cream cheese with an electric mixer for 4-5 minutes or until smooth. Add the lemon zest, vanilla and dextrose and beat until well combined.

5   Whisk the cream until soft peaks form, then gently fold through the cream cheese mixture until well combined. Spoon onto the cooked base in the tin and smooth the top. Refrigerate for 4-6 hours or until set. Store in an airtight container in the fridge for up to 2 days.

CHOCOLATE MOUSSE TART

SERVES 6-8

1 teaspoon powdered gelatine

¼ cup warm water

½ cup dextrose

¼ cup cocoa powder, sifted, plus extra for dusting

1 cup pouring cream

1 teaspoon vanilla essence, or to taste

whipped cream (optional), to serve

Chocolate pastry

½ cup plain flour, sifted

¼ cup cocoa powder, sifted

⅓ cup desiccated coconut

⅓ cup dextrose

100 g unsalted butter, melted

- - - - - - - - - - - - - - - - - -

» VARIATION:

If you like, replace the vanilla essence with a few drops of natural peppermint essence for a choc-mint flavoured tart.

Although this tart is not overly sweet, for sugar-free converts the luscious texture and decadent chocolate-y flavour of this mousse tart is guaranteed to tempt you.

1 Preheat the oven to 170°C (150°C fan-forced). Grease a 20 cm pie tin or deep tart tin with a removable base.

2 To make the chocolate pastry, process the flour, cocoa, coconut, dextrose and butter in a food processor until the mixture just comes together to form a dough. Press into the base and side of the prepared tart tin.

3 Bake the pastry for 20-25 minutes or until dry and dark brown. Leave to cool completely.

4 Meanwhile, place the gelatine in a small jug and pour over the warm water. Whisk with a fork until the gelatine has dissolved. Set aside for 1 minute.

5 Mix the dextrose and cocoa in a bowl. Add the cream and vanilla and whisk until soft peaks form. Add the gelatine mixture and whisk gently until well combined. Spoon into the cooled tart shell and refrigerate for 2-3 hours or until set. Top with whipped cream, if desired, then dust with extra cocoa and serve.

BAKLAVA

MAKES 18 PIECES

150 g walnuts

150 g peeled pistachios

¼ cup dextrose

1 teaspoon ground cinnamon

180 g unsalted butter, melted and cooled

1 × 375 g packet filo pastry (it is impossible to buy filo that doesn't contain vegetable oil; however, you won't consume a significant quantity when you eat a few pieces of this)

2 teaspoons water

Clove syrup

1 cup glucose syrup

¾ cup dextrose

½ cup water

finely grated zest of 1 lemon

6 cloves

- - - - - - - - - - - - - - - - - - - -

» VARIATION:

If you don't have any whole cloves in your pantry use a cinnamon stick instead to make a cinnamon syrup.

The trick to making this is to buy refrigerated filo pastry.

1   To make the syrup, bring the glucose, dextrose, water, lemon zest and cloves to the boil in a saucepan over high heat, stirring until the dextrose has dissolved. Reduce the heat to medium and simmer for 3–5 minutes. Set aside to cool.

2   Preheat the oven to 180°C (160°C fan-forced). Toast the walnuts on a baking tray for 5–8 minutes or until golden. Cool. Process the walnuts, pistachios, dextrose and cinnamon in a food processor until finely chopped.

3   Brush a 30 cm × 20 cm baking tin with butter. Unroll the filo on a chopping board and place the prepared tin on top. Use a small sharp knife to cut around the top of the tin all the way through the filo sheets. Discard the trimmings. Keep the filo covered with a clean, slightly damp tea towel to stop it from drying out.

4   Brush 1 filo sheet at a time with butter, then put into the tin. Repeat to create 9 layers of filo. Evenly scatter over one-third of the nut mixture. Repeat the buttering and layering process with another 6 filo sheets. Scatter over another third of the nuts and top with another 6 buttered and layered filo sheets. Scatter over the remaining nuts, then top with another 6 buttered filo sheets. Brush the top with melted butter. Freeze for 10 minutes, then use a small, sharp knife to score the top layers of filo in a diamond pattern and sprinkle the top with the water.

5   Bake the baklava for 30–35 minutes or until golden. Pour the syrup over the hot baklava and set aside to cool at room temperature for 2 hours. Cut to serve. This is best eaten on the day it is made.

DESS

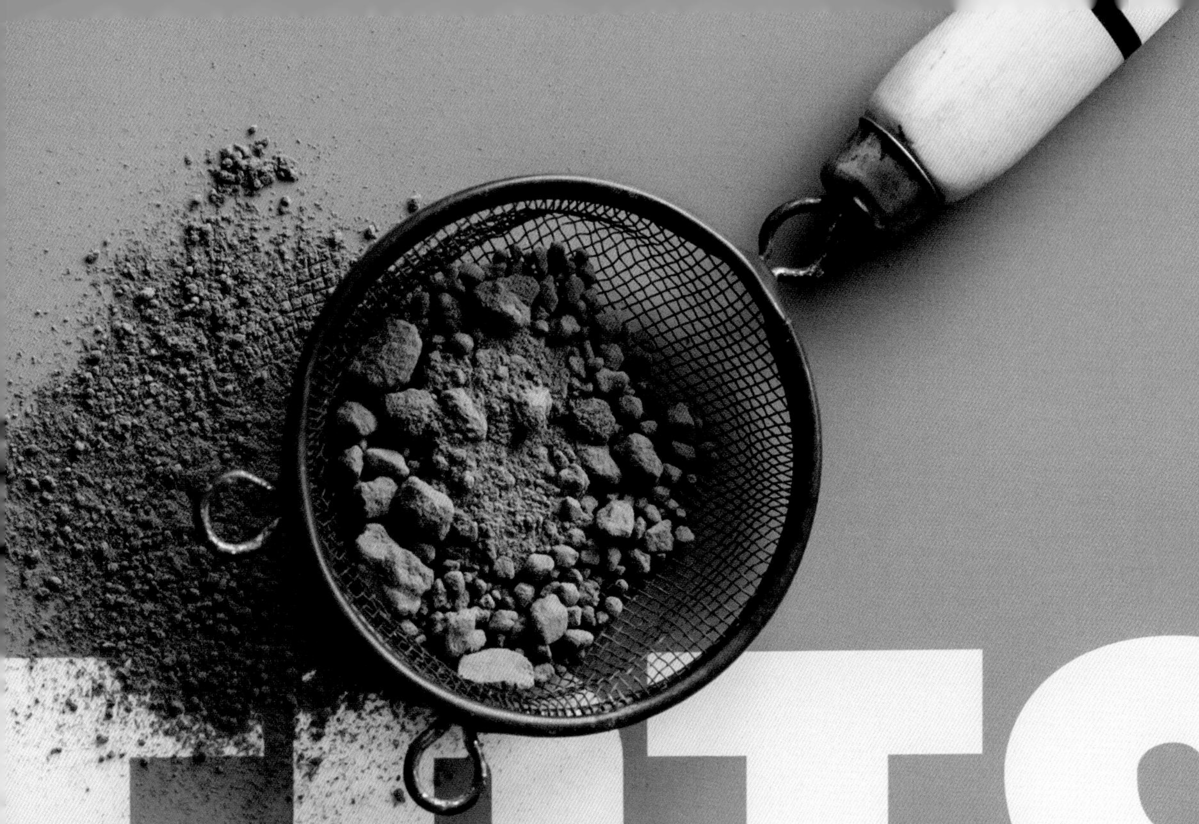

ERTS

CHOCOLATE PROFITEROLES

MAKES 18

1 cup water
80 g unsalted butter, chopped
1 cup plain flour, sifted
3 eggs

Vanilla cream
1 cup thickened cream
⅓ cup dextrose
1 teaspoon vanilla essence,
  or to taste

Chocolate glaze
¼ cup cocoa powder, sifted
1 cup dextrose
2 tablespoons boiling water

These gorgeous little choux pastry treats are so delicious that even sugar addicts won't know they are sugar-free! Profiteroles are best eaten on the day they are made.

1 Preheat the oven to 200°C (180°C fan-forced). Line 2 baking trays with baking paper.

2 Put the water and butter into a saucepan over high heat. Cook for 5 minutes or until the butter has melted and the mixture comes to the boil. Add the flour and beat with a wooden spoon until smooth. Cook the paste over low heat, stirring constantly for 2-3 minutes or until it comes away from the side of the pan. Remove the pan from the heat and add one egg at a time, beating with the wooden spoon after adding each one until the eggs are incorporated.

3 Spoon the choux pastry into a piping bag fitted with a 1 cm nozzle. Pipe 4 cm rounds onto the prepared trays. Bake for 20-25 minutes or until puffed and golden. Transfer to wire racks to cool completely.

4 To make the vanilla cream, whisk the cream, dextrose and vanilla in a bowl until soft peaks form. Make a small incision in each profiterole with a sharp knife, then spoon a tablespoon of the cream mixture into the centre.

5 To make the chocolate glaze, mix the cocoa, dextrose and water in a heatproof bowl, stirring until smooth. Dip the top of each profiterole into the glaze, then serve.

POACHED PEARS WITH BRIE

SERVES 4

2 cups dextrose
1.5 litres water
4 beurre bosc pears
1 vanilla bean, split and
    seeds scraped
ripe brie, to serve

Use this versatile syrup to poach your favourite seasonal fruit. The trick to poaching is to keep your liquid at a gentle simmer. Don't let it boil or your fruit will not cook evenly and keep its shape.

1   Put the dextrose and water into a saucepan. Stir over medium heat until the dextrose has dissolved. Simmer for 5 minutes or until the syrup has thickened slightly.

2   Peel the pears from the stem down, if you like. Add the pears and vanilla bean to the syrup. Cover with a piece of baking paper, then simmer over low heat for 15–20 minutes or until the pears are tender when tested with a skewer, turning occasionally to ensure even cooking.

3   Serve the pears warm or cooled with a little poaching liquid and soft brie alongside.

» VARIATION:

Add whatever flavour you like to the syrup. If you're poaching plums, I suggest popping a drop of rosewater into the syrup. (Leave the skin of the fruit on for more fibre.)

CHOCOLATE FONDANTS

SERVES 6

250 g unsalted butter, chopped
½ cup cocoa powder,
  plus extra for dusting
5 eggs
5 egg yolks
2 cups dextrose
1⅔ cups plain flour, sifted
double cream, to serve (optional)

Making gooey chocolate fondants without using purchased chocolate has been a little tricky. However, through lots of experimenting we've discovered that the butter and cocoa in this mixture successfully recreate the soft, oozing chocolate 'volcano' experience you expect from a fondant.

1 Preheat the oven to 160°C (140°C fan-forced). Grease and flour six 1 cup-capacity ramekins.

2 Put the butter and cocoa into a heatproof bowl over a saucepan of boiling water and stir until melted and well combined, making sure the bottom of the bowl doesn't touch the water. Set aside to cool slightly.

3 Whisk the eggs, egg yolks and dextrose with an electric mixer until light and creamy. Pour the butter mixture into the egg mixture and stir to combine well. Gently fold in the flour until well combined. Spoon evenly into the prepared ramekins and set aside for 5-10 minutes.

4 Line the base of a large roasting tin with a tea towel folded to fit. Place the ramekins on the tea towel. Pour enough boiling water into the tin to reach halfway up the sides of the ramekins. Cover the roasting tin with foil.

5 Bake the fondants for 35-40 minutes or until the tops are cooked but the mixture is still soft in the centre. Remove the ramekins from the roasting tin and leave to set for 15 minutes. Dust generously with extra cocoa and serve with double cream, if desired.

PAVLOVA WITH BERRIES & PASSIONFRUIT

SERVES 6-8

olive oil spray, for greasing
4 egg whites
1 cup dextrose
3 teaspoons cornflour
1 teaspoon white vinegar
1 cup thickened cream, whipped
125 g strawberries, hulled and halved
125 g raspberries
2-3 passionfruit, halved and pulp removed

- - - - - - - - - - - - - - - - - - - -

» VARIATION:

Add a few drops of natural rosewater essence to the whipped cream for a rose-scented pavlova.

It is tricky to make pavlova without using sugar. After much experimenting, we've found it's really a matter of taking care not to over-beat the egg whites and allowing the meringue to dry out completely in the oven after turning the oven off. The extra cornflour also adds stability to the meringue. However, if your pavlova doesn't turn out picture-perfect, all is not lost – simply smash the meringue and serve it in glasses or cups with the cream and fruit for a delicious Eton mess.

1   Preheat the oven to 150°C (130° fan-forced). Draw an 18 cm round on a piece of baking paper, then put the paper upside-down onto a lightly sprayed baking tray.

2   Beat the egg whites with an electric mixer until soft peaks just form - do not over-beat. With the motor running, gradually add the dextrose, beating well until the meringue is glossy. Sift the cornflour over, then gently fold in the vinegar.

3   Mound the meringue onto the baking paper on the marked round. Put the baking tray into the oven, then immediately reduce the oven temperature to 120°C (100°C fan-forced) and bake for 1 hour. Turn the oven off, then leave the meringue inside to cool completely.

4   Just before serving, transfer the meringue to a plate, then top with the whipped cream, berries and passionfruit pulp. Serve immediately. Pavlova is best eaten on the day it is made.

CREME CARAMEL

MAKES 4

1¼ cups dextrose
¾ cup milk
½ cup thickened cream
2 eggs
1 egg yolk
2 tablespoons glucose syrup

The oozing caramel coating of this luscious custard always impresses when it appears on the dinner table.

1 Preheat the oven to 190°C (170°C fan-forced).

2 Put 1 cup of the dextrose into a large frying pan. Stir over medium heat for 3-5 minutes until the dextrose has dissolved and turned golden. Pour evenly into four ½ cup-capacity ramekins. Set aside.

3 Put the milk and cream into a medium saucepan. Bring just to the boil over medium heat. Remove from the heat.

4 Whisk the eggs, egg yolk, glucose and remaining dextrose in a large heatproof bowl until well combined. Gradually whisk in the milk mixture and carefully pour evenly into the ramekins.

5 Line the base of a large roasting tin with a tea towel folded to fit. Place the ramekins on the tea towel. Pour enough boiling water into the tin to reach halfway up the sides of the ramekins. Cover the roasting tin with foil.

6 Bake the custards for 40-45 minutes or until they are just set. Remove the ramekins from the tin and set aside for 2 hours to cool. Refrigerate for 2-3 hours.

7 To unmould, run a flat-bladed knife around the inside edge of each ramekin and carefully turn out each creme caramel onto a shallow bowl or serving plate. Serve.

- -

» VARIATION:

To make a coconut version of creme caramel to top off an Asian-themed dinner party, replace the thickened cream with coconut cream and add some finely grated lime zest.

PASSIONFRUIT SOUFFLES

SERVES 6

melted butter, for greasing

100 g dextrose, plus extra for dusting

150 ml passionfruit pulp (from about 7 passionfruit)

1 tablespoon cornflour

3 teaspoons water

5 egg whites

Surprise your guests with these perfect passionfruit souffles – they never fail to impress.

1   Preheat the oven to 180°C (160°C fan-forced). Brush six 1 cup-capacity ramekins generously with melted butter, then dust generously with extra dextrose and put onto a baking tray.

2   Put the passionfruit pulp and ¼ cup of the dextrose into a small saucepan. Stir over low heat until the dextrose has dissolved. Increase the heat to high and bring to the boil.

3   Mix the cornflour and water in a small bowl to form a smooth paste. Remove the pan from the heat and whisk in the cornflour paste. Return the pan to the heat and cook, whisking continuously, for 1 minute. Transfer the mixture to a bowl and refrigerate until cold.

4   Whisk the egg whites with an electric mixer until foamy. Gradually add the remaining dextrose and continue to whisk just until stiff peaks form. Add a large spoonful of egg white to the passionfruit mixture and stir with a large metal spoon until combined to loosen the mixture. Gently fold in the remaining egg white.

5   Fill the ramekins to the top with the souffle mixture and run a palette knife across the top to make a flat surface. Run your thumb around the inside of the rim of each ramekin to help the souffles rise evenly.

6   Bake the souffles for 10-12 minutes or until risen and golden. Serve immediately.

BERRY CRUMBLE

SERVES 6-8

250 g raspberries

250 g blueberries

1½ cups dextrose

1 tablespoon vanilla essence,
  or to taste

1 tablespoon finely grated
  lemon zest

double cream, to serve (optional)

Crumble topping

½ cup ground almonds

1½ cups plain flour

1 cup dextrose

½ cup flaked almonds

180 g unsalted butter, melted

- - - - - - - - - - - - - - - - - - - -

》 VARIATION:

Crumble can be made with
any fruit that is in season,
such as apples, pears, plums
or rhubarb.

Who doesn't love the appealing contrast of a soft fruit
base and crisp topping that a crumble offers? Now you
can be transported back to your childhood with this
sugar-free topping.

1 Preheat the oven to 170°C (150°C fan-forced).

2 Put the berries, dextrose, vanilla and lemon zest into a saucepan
   over medium heat and stir for 5 minutes or until the berries have
   softened but still hold their shape. Transfer to a 1 litre-capacity
   baking dish.

3 To make the crumble topping, mix the ground almonds, flour,
   dextrose, almonds and butter in a bowl, using your fingertips
   to rub in the butter until the mixture resembles very coarse
   crumbs. Scatter the crumble mixture evenly over the berries.

4 Bake the crumble for 30 minutes or until the topping is golden
   and cooked through. Serve with double cream, if desired.

CINNAMON & ORANGE SYLLABUB

SERVES 4

1 cup dry white wine

1 cup dextrose

zest of 1 orange, removed in thick strips with a vegetable peeler

1 cinnamon stick

300 ml pouring cream

orange segments (optional), to serve

Syllabub is a creamy English dessert traditionally made with wine, but you could flavour it with rum if you like. Just be careful not to over-beat your cream – soft peaks is all you need for this luscious dessert.

1 Put the wine, dextrose, orange zest and cinnamon into a medium saucepan. Bring to the boil over high heat, stirring until the dextrose has dissolved. Reduce the heat to medium and cook for 5–6 minutes. Remove from the heat and cool completely. Reserve ¼ cup of the syrup for drizzling. Remove and discard the orange zest and cinnamon.

2 Whisk the cream until soft peaks form. Fold in the remaining syrup and spoon into four 1 cup-capacity glasses. Serve topped with orange segments and drizzled with reserved syrup, if you like.

BAKED CUSTARD

SERVES 4-6

2½ cups milk

2 teaspoons vanilla essence,
or to taste

3 eggs

1 egg yolk

⅓ cup dextrose

1 nutmeg, freshly grated or
1 teaspoon ground nutmeg

This old-fashioned favourite will win new fans with its silky, soft and creamy texture – comfort food at its best.

1 Preheat the oven to 160°C (140°C fan-forced).

2 Put the milk and vanilla into a small heavy-based saucepan. Bring just to the boil over medium heat.

3 Whisk the eggs, egg yolk and dextrose in a large heatproof bowl until the dextrose has dissolved. Gradually whisk in the warm milk until well combined.

4 Pour the custard into a shallow 1.5 litre-capacity baking dish, then sprinkle with nutmeg. Place in a large roasting tin. Pour enough boiling water into the tin to reach halfway up the sides of the dish.

5 Bake the custard for 40-45 minutes or until the top is golden but the custard has a soft wobble. Set aside for 10 minutes to set. Serve warm.

- - - - - - - - - - - - - - - - - -

» VARIATION:

You can add a sliced banana or two to the base of the baking dish before pouring in the custard mixture.

CHOCOLATE-SWIRL RICE PUDDING

SERVES 4

1 cup arborio rice
1 litre milk
½ cup dextrose
1 vanilla bean, split and seeds scraped
1 cup chopped Sugar-free Chocolate (see page 168)

This simple rice pudding is flavoured with a swirl of homemade chocolate, which needs to be made a few hours in advance to allow time for it to set. You can leave this out and use fruit stewed with dextrose or the caramel sauce on page 67 instead. You can also try swirling through a spoonful or two of the strawberry jam on page 190 – it's delicious!

1 Put the rice, milk, dextrose and vanilla into a medium saucepan. Bring to the boil over high heat. Reduce the heat to low, then cover and cook, stirring occasionally, for 25-30 minutes or until the rice is tender. Remove the vanilla bean.

2 Stir in the chopped chocolate until just melted. Serve warm.

GINGER & VANILLA BRULEE

SERVES 6-8

600 ml thickened cream
1 vanilla bean, split
1 tablespoon ground ginger,
  or to taste
1 cardamom pod, bruised
1 cinnamon stick
6 egg yolks
1 cup dextrose

This is a more sophisticated version of the traditional baked custard on page 108. If you are not so keen on ginger, replace it with 2 teaspoons of ground nutmeg instead. You will need to use a kitchen blowtorch to caramelise the top of the brulee – don't use the oven griller as the custard will curdle.

1 Preheat the oven to 170°C (150°C fan-forced).

2 Put the cream, vanilla bean, ginger, cardamom and cinnamon into a saucepan. Bring just to the boil over medium heat.

3 Beat the egg yolks and ½ cup of the dextrose with an electric mixer for 5-6 minutes or until pale and doubled in volume. Strain the cream mixture, discarding the spices. Whisk the cream mixture into the egg yolk mixture until well combined.

4 Pour the custard into a 1.5 litre-capacity baking dish and place in a roasting tin. Carefully pour enough boiling water into the pan to come halfway up the side of the dish. Cover the tin with foil.

5 Bake the custard for 35-40 minutes or until it is cooked but still has a slight wobble. Remove the baking dish from the roasting tin and leave to cool completely.

6 Sprinkle the remaining dextrose over the cooled custard and use a kitchen blowtorch to caramelise the dextrose until the top is golden and crisp. Serve immediately.

» VARIATION:
  To make individual brulees use eight ½ cup-capacity ramekins instead and reduce the cooking time to 30-40 minutes.

BREAD & BUTTER PUDDING

SERVES 6

6 leftover Finger Buns (see page 151), sliced

50 g unsalted butter, softened

6 eggs, lightly beaten

1 cup milk

½ cup pouring cream

½ cup dextrose

cocoa powder, for dusting (optional)

Comfort food to warm the soul – and a terrific way to use up leftover finger buns. All recipes using custard should be cooked in a water bath to ensure a nice creamy and smooth texture.

1 Preheat the oven to 160°C (140°C fan-forced).

2 Put the sliced finger buns onto a clean surface and spread evenly with the butter. Arrange, buttered-side up, in a 1.5 litre-capacity baking dish in overlapping rows.

3 Whisk the eggs, milk, cream and dextrose in a large bowl. Strain through a fine sieve into a jug. Pour evenly over the finger bun slices. Set aside for 15 minutes to soak.

4 Put the baking dish into a large roasting tin. Pour enough boiling water into the tin to come halfway up the side of the baking dish.

5 Bake the pudding for 35–40 minutes or until the custard has just set. Dust with cocoa, if desired, then serve warm.

» VARIATION:

If you happen to have made the sugar-free chocolate on page 168, then roughly chop some and add it to the mixture before baking.

STICKY TOFFEE PUDDINGS

MAKES 4

75 g unsalted butter, melted
½ cup dextrose
2 eggs, lightly beaten
1 cup ground almonds
1 cup plain flour, sifted
1 teaspoon baking powder
⅓ cup milk
1 teaspoon vanilla essence,
  or to taste

Toffee syrup
1½ cups dextrose
50 g unsalted butter, chopped
2 tablespoons thickened cream

If you are a fan of toffee, you will really enjoy these indulgent little puddings, perfect for a quick mid-week pick-me-up after dinner.

1 Preheat the oven to 180°C (160°C fan-forced). Grease four 1 cup-capacity ovenproof moulds or ramekins.

2 Mix the butter, dextrose, egg, ground almonds, flour, baking powder, milk and vanilla in a large bowl until smooth and well combined.

3 Spoon the batter evenly into the prepared moulds or ramekins, then put onto a baking tray to catch any overflowing syrup.

4 Bake the puddings for 30–35 minutes or until the tops are golden and the puddings are cooked through when tested with a skewer.

5 Meanwhile, to make the toffee syrup, put the dextrose into a large frying pan and cook over medium heat for 2 minutes or until melted and golden. Carefully whisk in the butter and the cream until well combined and smooth, then pour over the puddings immediately. Serve hot.

FIVE-MINUTE CHOCOLATE CUP PUDDINGS

MAKES 4

½ cup milk

⅓ cup olive oil

1 tablespoon vanilla essence,
   or to taste

2 eggs

⅔ cup dextrose

½ cup self-raising flour, sifted

¼ cup cocoa powder, sifted,
   plus extra for dusting

whipped cream, to serve

I really love this pudding. It's just the thing for when you're looking for a quick chocolate hit but don't have the time or inclination to make anything too complicated. Just be careful not to overcook it or you'll lose the luscious texture.

1 Whisk the milk, oil, vanilla and eggs in a bowl until smooth. Add the dextrose, flour and cocoa and whisk until well combined and smooth.

2 Pour into four 1 cup-capacity microwave-safe mugs or tea cups. Cook in the microwave on medium power for 1 minute or until just cooked. Dust with extra cocoa, then top with a spoonful of cream and serve.

» VARIATION:
For jaffa-flavoured puddings, stir some finely grated orange zest into the batter before cooking.

CHERRY TRIFLE

SERVES 6-8

110 g unsalted butter, chopped and softened

½ cup dextrose, plus extra for dusting

1 teaspoon vanilla essence, or to taste

2 eggs

⅔ cup self-raising flour, sifted

2 tablespoons cornflour, sifted

2 tablespoons milk

1 cup pouring cream, whipped

1 quantity Poached Cherries (see page 192)

cherries (optional), to serve

Vanilla custard

2 cups pouring cream

1 cup milk

1 teaspoon vanilla essence, or to taste

6 egg yolks

1½ cups dextrose

- - - - - - - - - - - - - - - - - - - -

» VARIATION:

Try flavouring the custard with ground spices such as cinnamon or cloves or stir in some cocoa powder for a chocolate custard.

1 Preheat the oven to 180°C (160°C fan-forced). Grease and line two 18 cm springform cake tins with baking paper.

2 Beat the butter, dextrose and vanilla with an electric mixer until light and creamy. Add one egg at a time, beating well after adding each one. Fold in the flour and cornflour until well combined. Fold in the milk. Spoon the batter into the prepared tins.

3 Bake the cakes for 20-25 minutes or until they pull away from the edges of the tins. Leave to cool in the tins for 10 minutes, then turn out onto wire racks to cool completely.

4 To make the custard, put the cream, milk and vanilla into a heavy-based saucepan. Bring just to the boil over medium heat. Whisk the egg yolks and dextrose in a large heatproof bowl until the dextrose has dissolved. Gradually whisk the cream mixture into the egg yolk mixture until well combined. Transfer the custard to a clean heavy-based saucepan and cook over medium heat, stirring continuously, for 8-10 minutes or until the mixture is thick enough to coat the back of a spoon. Strain into a bowl, cover closely with plastic film and refrigerate until cold.

5 To assemble, cut the sponges in half widthways. Put one layer of sponge into a 1.5 litre-capacity glass dish (mine is 20 cm round). Top with some of the custard, another layer of sponge and some of the cream, then top with the poached cherries and their syrup. Top the cherries with another layer of sponge and custard, then finish with the final layer of cake and cream.

6 Set aside for 2 hours to allow the flavours to soak into the sponge (refrigerate if it's a hot day). Serve, topped with fresh cherries, if you like.

EASTER
TREATS

ICE CR

SOR

& JELL

EAMS
BET
LIES

ICE CREAM SUNDAES WITH PISTACHIO TOFFEE

MAKES 1 LITRE

2 cups pouring cream

1 cup milk

1 teaspoon vanilla essence,
  or to taste

¼ cup glucose syrup

6 egg yolks

1 cup dextrose

1 quantity Hot Chocolate Fudge
  Sauce (see page 191)

Pistachio toffee

1 cup dextrose

½ cup pistachios, chopped

Use this vanilla-scented custard base to make any flavoured ice cream you like. The pistachio toffee adds a crunchy texture, but you can simply top the sundaes with pistachios.

1   Put the cream, milk and vanilla into a heavy-based saucepan and bring just to the boil over medium heat. Stir through the glucose until dissolved and well combined.

2   Whisk the egg yolks and dextrose in a large bowl until the dextrose has dissolved. Gradually whisk in the cream mixture until well combined.

3   Transfer the custard mixture to a clean saucepan and cook over medium heat, stirring continuously, for 8–10 minutes or until the mixture is thick enough to coat the back of a spoon. Strain into a bowl, cover closely with plastic film and refrigerate until cold.

4   Transfer the custard mixture to an ice-cream machine and churn according to the manufacturer's directions until frozen. Spoon into a 1 litre-capacity loaf tin and freeze for 2–3 hours or until hard. (Alternatively, you can scoop it directly from the ice-cream machine if you like soft-serve ice cream.)

5   To make the pistachio toffee, put the dextrose into a large non-stick frying pan and cook over medium heat for 4–5 minutes or until melted and golden. Pour onto a baking tray lined with baking paper, sprinkle over the pistachios and leave to cool for 10 minutes or until crisp. Break into large pieces.

6   Scoop the ice cream into sundae glasses or serving bowls, then top with the hot fudge sauce and pistachio toffee. Serve.

RHUBARB CRUMBLE ICE CREAM

MAKES 1 LITRE

250 g rhubarb stalks,
cut into 5 cm lengths

2 cups dextrose

1 cup pouring cream

1 cup sour cream

1 cup milk

1 teaspoon vanilla essence,
or to taste

6 egg yolks

Almond crumble

¼ cup ground almonds

¾ cup plain flour

½ cup dextrose

90 g unsalted butter, melted

— — — — — — — — — — — — — —

》 VARIATION:

In addition to, or instead of, rhubarb, you could stir through raspberries, blueberries or any slightly softened fruit you like.

Your guests will love the contrasting textures of this sweet-and-sour ice cream with a crunchy crumble topping.

1 Preheat the oven to 160°C (140°C fan-forced). Line a baking tray with baking paper.

2 To make the almond crumble, mix the almonds, flour, dextrose and butter in a medium bowl until the mixture resembles very coarse breadcrumbs. Spread out on the prepared tray and bake for 15–20 minutes or until golden. Set aside to cool.

3 Put the rhubarb and 1 cup of the dextrose into a medium saucepan. Cook over medium heat for 5–8 minutes or until the rhubarb has softened. Transfer to a bowl and leave to cool.

4 Put the cream, sour cream, milk and vanilla into a heavy-based saucepan. Bring just to the boil over medium heat. Whisk the egg yolks and remaining dextrose in a large bowl until the dextrose has dissolved. Gradually whisk in the cream mixture until well combined. Transfer to a clean saucepan and cook over medium heat, stirring continuously for 8–10 minutes or until the mixture is thick enough to coat the back of a spoon. Strain into a bowl, cover closely with plastic film and refrigerate until cold.

5 Transfer the custard to an ice-cream machine and churn according to manufacturer's directions until frozen. Add the rhubarb to the ice-cream machine and continue to churn for 5 minutes or until well combined. Transfer to a 1 litre-capacity loaf tin lined with plastic film and smooth the top. Top with the crumble, then wrap with plastic film and freeze for 2 hours or until set. Store in the freezer for up to 1 week.

VANILLA YOGHURT & PASSIONFRUIT JELLIES

MAKES 8

500 g natural yoghurt (I use Jalna Biodynamic yoghurt)

¼ cup dextrose

2 teaspoons vanilla essence, or to taste

2 tablespoons water

2 teaspoons powdered gelatine

Passionfruit jelly

12 passionfruit, halved and pulp removed

¼ cup water

2 tablespoons dextrose

2 teaspoons powdered gelatine

Make this pretty dessert ahead of time for a dinner party or simply to have in the fridge for cooling mid-week snacks and desserts.

1   Whisk together the yoghurt, dextrose and vanilla in a medium bowl. Put the water into a small jug and sprinkle over the gelatine. Set aside for 5 minutes to dissolve. Whisk the gelatine mixture into the yoghurt mixture. Spoon evenly into eight 1 cup-capacity serving glasses. Refrigerate for 2 hours or until set.

2   To make the passionfruit jelly, put the passionfruit pulp, water and dextrose into a saucepan. Bring just to the boil. Remove from the heat and stir in the gelatine until dissolved. Spoon evenly over the set yoghurt jellies, then refrigerate for 2 hours or until set. Serve.

COCONUT & LIME SORBET

SERVES 4

1½ cups dextrose

2 cups water

1 lime, zest removed in wide strips with a vegetable peeler

2 cups coconut milk

Living in Queensland it gets very steamy during summer. It's great to have a refreshing iced treat like this in the freezer to cool down on those balmy summer days – and nights.

1   Put the dextrose, water and lime zest into a medium saucepan. Stir over low heat until the dextrose has dissolved. Increase the heat to medium and simmer for 5 minutes. Stir in the coconut milk. Remove from the heat and cool completely.

2   Pour into an ice-cream machine and churn according to manufacturer's directions until frozen. Spoon into 4 glasses to serve. Store in an airtight container in the freezer for up to 2 weeks.

» VARIATION:

If you do not have an ice cream machine, use hand-held electric beaters to beat the sorbet every 2 hours, returning the mixture to the freezer each time, until the mixture is frozen.

ROCKMELON ICY POLES

MAKES 8

These icy poles can be made with any pureed whole fruit you or your kids like.

½ cup dextrose
½ cup water
1 lime, zest removed in wide strips
1 large rockmelon (cantaloupe), peeled, seeded and chopped

1   Put the dextrose, water and lime zest into a small saucepan. Stir the mixture over high heat until the dextrose has dissolved. Transfer to a bowl and refrigerate for 1 hour or until cold. Strain and discard the lime zest.

2   Blend the rockmelon in a food processor until a smooth puree forms. Add the dextrose syrup and blend until well combined.

3   Divide the rockmelon mixture among 8 icy-pole moulds. Put into the freezer overnight or until frozen. Store in the freezer for up to 1 month.

- -

» VARIATION:

If you don't have icy pole moulds, simply put the icy pole mixture into glasses sprayed with olive oil spray or disposable cups and place a paddle pop stick in the middle.

MILKY-WAY ICY POLES

MAKES 6

Kids both big and small will love these creamy treats.

2½ cups milk
1 tablespoon cornflour
1 teaspoon vanilla essence, or to taste
½ cup dextrose
½ cup thickened cream

1   Whisk ¼ cup of the milk and the cornflour in a small bowl until the cornflour has dissolved.

2   Put the vanilla and remaining milk into a small saucepan. Bring just to the boil over medium heat. Add the cornflour mixture and dextrose and cook, stirring for 4–5 minutes. Add the cream and stir until well combined.

3   Transfer the mixture to a heatproof bowl, then cover with plastic film and refrigerate until cold.

4   Divide among 6 icy pole moulds. Put into the freezer overnight or until frozen. Store in the freezer for up to 1 month.

CHOCOLATE ICE CREAM CONES

MAKES 10

2 cups pouring cream

1 cup milk

1 teaspoon vanilla essence,
   or to taste

¼ cup glucose syrup

6 egg yolks

1 cup dextrose

¼ cup cocoa powder, sifted

Chocolate cones

100 g unsalted butter, chopped
   and softened

1 cup dextrose

4 egg whites, lightly beaten

½ cup plain flour, sifted

¼ cup cocoa powder, sifted

- - - - - - - - - - - - - - - - - -

》 VARIATION:

Push the hot waffles into muffin
tin holes to make tuille baskets
for your ice cream.

If you're short of time, you could just make the ice cream
and serve it in bowls – I'm sure you won't get any complaints!

1   Put the cream, milk and vanilla into a heavy-based saucepan.
    Bring just to the boil over medium heat. Stir in the glucose until
    melted and well combined.

2   Whisk the egg yolks, dextrose and cocoa in a large bowl until the
    dextrose has dissolved. Gradually whisk in the cream mixture
    until well combined. Transfer to a clean saucepan and cook over
    medium heat, stirring continuously, for 8–10 minutes or until the
    mixture is thick enough to coat the back of a spoon. Strain into
    a bowl, cover closely with plastic film and refrigerate until cold.

3   Pour into an ice-cream machine and churn and freeze according
    to the manufacturer's instructions.

4   To make the cones, preheat the oven to 180°C (160°C fan-
    forced). Grease and line a baking tray with baking paper.

5   Beat the butter and dextrose with an electric mixer until light and
    creamy. With the motor running, gradually add the egg whites,
    flour and cocoa and continue to beat until a batter forms. Spoon
    2 teaspoons of the batter at a time onto the prepared tray and
    spread very thinly with a palette knife to form a round shape.
    Bake for 6–8 minutes or until cooked and dry. Working very
    quickly, curl each one around with your hands to form a cone.
    Set aside to cool. (Makes 10. If the waffle cones soften, freeze
    for an hour or so to crisp again.)

6   Scoop the ice cream into the cones and serve.

CHEAT'S VANILLA ICE CREAM & CHOCOLATE CHIP SANDWICHES

MAKES 8

2 cups milk

2 cups thickened cream

1¼ cups dextrose

4 egg yolks

2 teaspoons vanilla essence, or to taste

1 cup chopped Sugar-free Chocolate (see page 168)

16 wafers (available from the biscuit section of supermarkets)

cocoa powder, for dusting

I love how easy it is to make your own ice cream without having to start off by making a custard. However, this recipe uses raw eggs. If you're not comfortable with this, you can use the milk, cream, dextrose, egg yolks and vanilla to make a cooked custard base, following the instructions on page 134. These chocolate-studded ice cream sandwiches are a terrific way to use packaged wafers, which are almost sugar-free (0.02 grams per wafer). Unfortunately, the wafers also aren't free from seed oils, but you won't consume a significant quantity if you have a couple of these delicious sandwiches.

1   Whisk the milk, cream, dextrose, egg yolks and vanilla in a large bowl until smooth. Pour into an ice-cream machine and churn and freeze according to the manufacturer's directions. Stir in the chopped chocolate until well combined.

2   Put 8 wafers into a 30 cm × 20 cm slice tin, then cover with a thick layer of ice cream. Top with the remaining 8 wafers and put into the freezer for 2–3 hours or until frozen.

3   Use a knife to evenly trim the sandwiches and carefully separate them. Serve dusted with cocoa. Store any leftover sandwiches in an airtight container in the freezer for up to 1 month.

KIDS' LUNCH &

BOX
PARTY
FARE

BLUEBERRY & CINNAMON OAT SQUARES

MAKES 24 SQUARES

2 cups quick-cook oats
½ cup self-raising flour
½ cup desiccated coconut
125 g blueberries
2 teaspoons ground cinnamon
80 g unsalted butter, chopped
½ cup rice malt syrup
½ cup dextrose

This is one of my kids' favourites! Just make sure you allow the slice to cool at room temperature before cutting.

1 Preheat the oven to 180°C (160°C fan-forced). Grease and line a 30 cm × 20 cm slice tin with baking paper.

2 Mix the oats, flour, coconut, blueberries and cinnamon in a large bowl.

3 Put the butter, syrup and dextrose into a saucepan. Stir frequently over low heat for 6–8 minutes or until the butter has melted and mixture is well combined. Pour over the oat mixture. Stir until well combined. Spoon the mixture into the prepared tin, using damp hands or the back of a spoon to smooth the surface.

4 Bake the slice for 25–30 minutes or until golden. Cool completely in the tin. Cut into squares to serve. Store in an airtight container in the fridge for up to 2 days.

CHOCOLATE CRACKLES

MAKES 12

250 g cocoa butter
2⅔ cups puffed rice
¾ cup dextrose
2 tablespoons cocoa
   powder, sifted
¾ cup desiccated coconut

Quick and easy to make, this nostalgic treat is an all-time favourite for kids' birthday parties and cake stalls. Puffed rice is available from supermarkets and health food stores.

Copha works just as well as cocoa butter in this recipe, however, it does contain a small amount of transfats, so it's not an ideal choice. We don't often eat chocolate crackles – less than once a year – so we just use copha. But if you are tucking into them on a frequent basis, it's a good idea to switch to cocoa butter. You'll find it in most health food stores; however, be warned, it can be quite expensive.

1 Line twelve ½ cup-capacity muffin tin holes with paper cases.

2 Melt the cocoa butter in a saucepan over low heat. Mix the puffed rice, dextrose, cocoa and coconut in a bowl. Pour in the melted cocoa butter and stir until well combined.

3 Spoon the mixture evenly into the prepared paper cases. Refrigerate for 2 hours or until set. Store in an airtight container in the fridge for up to 4 days.

MARSHMALLOWS

MAKES ABOUT 30

2 cups dextrose

1⅓ cups water

2 tablespoons gelatine

1 teaspoon vanilla essence, or to taste

red food colouring, as needed (optional)

¼ cup cornflour

These fluffy marshmallows are a cinch to make with the kids. Serve them instead of lollies at a kid's party and watch them disappear.

1 Grease and line two 30 cm × 20 cm slice tins with baking paper.

2 Put 1½ cups of the dextrose and ⅔ cup of the water into a medium saucepan. Cook over medium heat, stirring frequently, for 3-5 minutes or until the dextrose has dissolved.

3 Put the gelatine and remaining ⅔ cup water into a jug and stir until the gelatine has dissolved. Carefully pour into the pan of hot dextrose syrup. Stir over medium heat for 2-3 minutes or until the gelatine has dissolved.

4 Beat the gelatine mixture and vanilla with an electric mixer for 8-10 minutes or until thick. Spoon half of the mixture into one of the prepared tins and smooth the top. Add a little red food colouring to the remaining mixture, if desired, then spoon into the second tin and smooth the top. Set aside at room temperature for 1 hour or until set.

5 Mix the cornflour and remaining dextrose in a small bowl until well combined.

6 Remove the marshmallow from the tins and use a 6 cm cookie cutter to cut it into 30 rounds. Put each marshmallow into the dextrose and cornflour mixture and roll gently to coat. Serve. Store in an airtight container in a cool, dry place for up to 2 days.

CINNAMON DOUGHNUTS

MAKES 10

2 teaspoons dried yeast

1½ tablespoons warm water

½ cup warm milk

2 tablespoons dextrose, plus
¼ cup extra for dusting

50 g unsalted butter, melted

2¼ cups plain flour, sifted, plus
extra for dusting

1 teaspoon ground nutmeg

2 eggs, lightly beaten

2 tablespoons ground cinnamon

800 g lard or solidified cooking
oil (blended animal fat), for
deep-frying

- - - - - - - - - - - - - - - - - -

» VARIATION:

To make iced donuts simply
omit the cinnamon coating and
ice with the chocolate glaze on
page 92 instead.

Hot doughnuts fresh out of the pan are one of life's special
treats and these cinnamon coated ones won't disappoint.

1   Put the yeast, water, milk and 1 tablespoon of the dextrose in
    a large bowl and set aside in a warm place for 10 minutes or
    until bubbles appear on the surface.

2   Add the butter, flour, nutmeg, egg and remaining dextrose to
    the yeast mixture and use a butter knife to mix until a sticky
    dough forms.

3   Turn out the dough onto a lightly floured surface and knead
    until smooth. Put the dough into a lightly oiled bowl, cover
    with a clean, damp tea towel and set aside in a warm place for
    45 minutes or until doubled in size. Meanwhile, mix the cinnamon
    and extra dextrose in a small bowl until well combined. Set aside.

4   Knead the dough on a lightly floured surface for 5 minutes or
    until smooth and elastic. Roll the dough into a log, then divide
    into 10 even portions and shape into rounds. Place the rounds
    on a baking tray lined with baking paper, cover with the tea
    towel and set aside for 30 minutes or until risen. Use the handle
    of a wooden spoon to poke a hole in the centre of each round.

5   Place the lard and a candy thermometer in a large deep saucepan
    over medium heat until the lard melts and registers 180°C on the
    thermometer. Cook the doughnuts, in batches, for 1-2 minutes on
    each side or until golden. Drain briefly on paper towel.

6   Dust the hot doughnuts with the cinnamon mixture and
    serve immediately.

BANANA BREAD

SERVES 8-10

1 cup dextrose

2 eggs

½ cup olive oil

2 teaspoons vanilla essence,
or to taste

1¼ cups plain flour, sifted

1 teaspoon bicarbonate of
soda, sifted

2 teaspoons ground cinnamon

2 bananas, mashed

80 g pecans (optional), toasted
and roughly chopped

butter (optional), to serve

- -

≫ VARIATION:

You can use walnuts or
hazelnuts instead of
pecans, if you prefer.

If you're making this for the kids' lunch-boxes or any
occasion where nut allergies may be an issue, simply
omit the pecans.

1   Preheat the oven to 170°C (150°C fan-forced). Grease and line
a 21 cm × 9 cm loaf tin with baking paper.

2   Beat the dextrose, eggs, oil and vanilla with an electric mixer
until light and creamy. Fold in the flour, bicarbonate of soda
and cinnamon until just combined. Fold in the banana and
pecans, if using. Spoon the batter into the prepared tin.

3   Bake the bread for 35-40 minutes or until cooked when tested
with a skewer. Cool in the tin for 5 minutes, then turn out onto
a wire rack to cool completely. Serve with butter, if desired.
Store leftover slices individually wrapped in plastic film or freezer
bags in an airtight container in the freezer for up to 1 month.

FINGER BUNS

MAKES 12

1 × 7g sachet dried yeast

⅓ cup dextrose

½ cup warm milk, plus extra
   for brushing

2½ cups plain flour, sifted, plus
   extra for dusting

1 teaspoon mixed spice

1 teaspoon ground cinnamon

50 g cold unsalted butter, chopped

1 egg, lightly beaten

1 teaspoon vanilla essence,
   or to taste

¼ cup warm water

1 quantity Egg-white Icing
   (see page 192)

⅓ cup desiccated coconut

» VARIATION:

You can add a few drops of red
food colouring to the icing, if
you like, to make pink icing.

Take a trip down memory lane with this old-fashioned
tuck-shop favourite. Leftover finger buns can be used
to make the bread and butter pudding on page 113.

1 Put the yeast, dextrose and warm milk into a heatproof jug and
set aside in a warm place for 10 minutes or until bubbles appear
on the surface.

2 Mix the flour, mixed spice and cinnamon in a large bowl until
well combined. Add the butter and rub it in with your fingertips
until the mixture resembles fine breadcrumbs. Make a well in the
centre, then add the egg, vanilla, warm water and yeast mixture
and mix until well combined.

3 Turn the dough out onto a lightly floured surface and knead
for 6–8 minutes or until smooth. Divide into twelve 13 cm-long
logs and put onto a baking tray lined with baking paper about
5 cm apart. Cover with a clean tea towel and leave to rest for
15 minutes.

4 Preheat the oven to 180°C (160° fan-forced).

5 Brush the tops of the finger buns with milk and bake for
12–15 minutes or until golden. Leave to cool completely.

6 Spread the icing onto the cooled finger buns, then sprinkle
with the coconut. Set aside for 2 hours for the icing to set.
Serve. Finger buns are best eaten on the day they are made.

APPLE & CINNAMON PIKELETS

MAKES 12

¾ cup self-raising flour, sifted
⅓ cup dextrose
2 eggs, lightly beaten
¾ cup milk
2 teaspoons vanilla essence, or to taste
2 unpeeled apples, grated
1 teaspoon ground cinnamon
butter, for pan-frying

Quick to cook, these are a welcome addition to the school lunch-box, either freshly made or frozen. Wrap any leftover pikelets in plastic film, then freeze in an airtight container to pop straight into the lunch-box from the freezer. The pikelets will thaw by recess.

1   Mix the flour and dextrose in a bowl. Make a well in the centre, then add the egg, milk and vanilla and whisk until a smooth batter forms. Stir in the apple and cinnamon, then set aside for 10 minutes.

2   Heat a little butter in a large non-stick frying pan over medium heat. Working in batches, add 2 tablespoons of the batter for each pikelet and cook for 2-3 minutes on each side or until golden and cooked through. Serve warm or at room temperature.

» VARIATION:

You could use grated pear instead of apple and replace the cinnamon with nutmeg or ground ginger.

CARROT CAKES WITH CREAM CHEESE ICING

MAKES 12

225 g unsalted butter, chopped
   and softened
1 cup dextrose
3 eggs
1¼ cups self-raising flour, sifted
1 teaspoon baking powder, sifted
2 teaspoons ground cinnamon
1 teaspoon ground ginger
¼ cup desiccated coconut
2 medium carrots, grated

Cream cheese icing
200 g cream cheese, softened
1 cup dextrose

- - - - - - - - - - - - - - - - - -

》 VARIATION:

Try adding a little finely grated orange zest to the cream cheese icing.

If you're new to living without fructose – or introducing fructose-free treats to your sugar-addicted family and friends – these sweet little cakes are a great way to start. The spices and coconut add loads of flavour.

1   Preheat the oven to 180°C (160°C fan-forced). Line a 12-hole muffin tin with paper cases.

2   Beat the butter and dextrose with an electric mixer until light and creamy. Add one egg at a time, beating well after adding each one, until the mixture is well combined.

3   Mix the flour, baking powder, cinnamon, ginger and coconut in a medium bowl. Add to the butter mixture and beat until just combined. Fold in the carrot. Spoon the batter evenly into the paper cases.

4   Bake the cakes for 25-30 minutes or until cooked when tested with a skewer. Transfer to a wire rack to cool completely.

5   To make the icing, beat the cream cheese and dextrose with an electric mixer until light and creamy.

6   Spread the icing onto the cooled carrot cakes and serve on the day they are made. Alternatively, store uniced cakes individually wrapped in plastic film or freezer bags in an airtight container in the freezer for up to 2 weeks.

CHOCOLATE COCONUT SLICE

MAKES 16

1 cup self-raising flour, sifted

1 cup dextrose

½ cup desiccated coconut, plus extra for sprinkling

1 tablespoon cocoa powder, sifted

125 g unsalted butter, melted

1 egg, lightly beaten

1 teaspoon vanilla essence, or to taste

Cocoa icing

1 cup dextrose

1 tablespoon cocoa powder

20 g unsalted butter, softened

1 tablespoon milk

» VARIATIONS:

Try adding some pecans or almonds for extra crunch if you don't have any nut allergies to worry about. Use gluten-free self-raising flour if your children are gluten-intolerant.

Enjoy this sugar-free version of a coconut rough in slice form!

1 Preheat the oven to 180°C (160°C fan-forced). Grease and line a 30 cm × 20 cm slice tin.

2 Mix the flour, dextrose, coconut and cocoa in a large bowl until well combined. Make a well in the centre, then add the butter, egg and vanilla and mix until well combined. Spoon into the prepared tin, then smooth the top.

3 Bake the slice for 20 minutes or until set. Leave in the tin to cool a little, then refrigerate for 2 hours or until completely cold.

4 Meanwhile, to make the icing, beat the dextrose, cocoa, butter and milk with an electric mixer until smooth and thick.

5 Spread the icing over the cold slice, then sprinkle with extra coconut. Cut into sixteen 9 cm × 3 cm bars. Serve. Store in an airtight container for up to 3 days.

BIRTHDAY TREATS

HOLI
TREA

AUSTRALIA DAY LAMINGTONS

MAKES 24

225 g unsalted butter, chopped and softened

1 cup dextrose, plus extra for dusting

1 teaspoon vanilla essence, or to taste

4 eggs

1⅓ cups self-raising flour, sifted

¼ cup cornflour, sifted

¼ cup milk

3–4 cups desiccated coconut, as needed

Chocolate icing

2 cups dextrose

¾ cup cocoa powder

¾ cup boiling water

50 g unsalted butter, melted

What could be more perfect to take to an Australia Day barbecue or picnic than these iconic little lamingtons? And no one will guess they don't contain sugar!

1 Preheat the oven to 180°C (160°C fan-forced). Grease and line a 30 cm × 20 cm slice tin with baking paper.

2 Beat the butter, dextrose and vanilla with an electric mixer until light and creamy. Add one egg at a time, beating well after adding each one; the mixture will look like it has split but it will be okay. Fold in the flour and cornflour until well combined. Fold in the milk. Spoon the batter into the prepared tin.

3 Bake the cake for 20–25 minutes or until cooked when tested with a skewer. Leave to cool in the tin for 10 minutes, then turn out onto a wire rack to cool completely.

4 To make the icing, put the dextrose, cocoa, boiling water and butter into a heatproof bowl, then whisk until smooth.

5 Trim the top and edges of the sponge with a large serrated knife, then cut into 4 widthways and 6 lengthways to yield 24 pieces. Gently roll each piece in extra dextrose, then in the icing to coat. Gently roll in the coconut to evenly coat all sides; use half of the coconut at a time to prevent it from becoming stained with the icing. Leave on a wire rack for the coating to set.

6 Serve on the day they are made or wrap individually in plastic film or freezer bags and store in an airtight container in the freezer for up to 2 weeks.

HOT CROSS BUNS

MAKES 12

4 cups plain flour, plus extra
    for dusting
1 tablespoon mixed spice
2 × 7g sachets dried yeast
¼ cup dextrose
pinch of salt
40 g unsalted butter
300 ml milk
2 eggs, lightly beaten
olive oil spray, for greasing

Flour paste
½ cup plain flour
90 ml water

Glaze
⅓ cup water
2 tablespoons dextrose

- - - - - - - - - - - - - - - -

» VARIATION:

If you like, knead some finely
grated orange zest into the
dough before baking.

If you love hot cross buns now you don't have to miss out.

1   Sift the flour and mixed spice into a large bowl, then add the
    yeast, dextrose and salt. Melt the butter in a small saucepan.
    Add the milk, then heat for 1 minute or until lukewarm. Add
    the warm milk mixture and egg to the flour mixture. Use a flat-
    bladed knife to mix until the dough almost comes together. Use
    clean hands to form a soft dough.

2   Knead the dough on a lightly floured surface for 5-10 minutes
    or until smooth. Transfer to a lightly oiled bowl. Cover with
    a clean tea towel. Set aside in a warm place for 1 hour or until
    doubled in size. Line a large baking tray with baking paper.

3   Punch the dough down to its original size. Knead on a lightly floured
    surface until smooth. Divide into 12 balls and put onto the prepared
    tray about 1 cm apart. Cover loosely with plastic film. Set aside in
    a warm place for 30 minutes or until doubled in size.

4   Preheat the oven to 200°C (180°C fan-forced).

5   For the paste, mix the flour and water until smooth, adding
    a little more water if needed. Spoon into a small snap-lock bag
    and snip off 1 corner. Pipe flour paste crosses on top of the buns.

6   Bake the hot cross buns for 15 minutes or until they are golden
    and cooked through.

7   For the glaze, stir the water and dextrose in a small saucepan
    over low heat until the dextrose has dissolved. Boil for 5 minutes.
    Brush the warm glaze over the warm hot cross buns. Serve.

CHOCOLATE EASTER NESTS

MAKES 16

250 g cocoa butter

2 cups shredded wheat
(I use Uncle Tobys),
roughly chopped

1 cup dextrose

2 tablespoons cocoa
powder, sifted

Let the kids help mix and shape these fun Easter nests.
They can be as creative as they like when the time comes
to decorate them. You can wrap them in cellophane as
your sugar-free contribution to an Easter egg hunt.

1 Line 2 baking trays with baking paper.

2 Melt the cocoa butter in a medium saucepan over low heat.

3 Put the shredded wheat, dextrose and cocoa into a medium
   bowl and mix until combined. Pour in the melted cocoa butter
   and stir until well combined.

4 Put tablespoons of the mixture onto the prepared trays.
   Use a teaspoon to push down in the centre to create the
   shape of a nest. Leave to cool and set at room temperature
   for 1 hour.

5 Decorate with small novelty chicks or other Easter-themed
   items, if desired. Store in an airtight container for up to 2 days.

>> VARIATION:

You could use copha instead
of cocoa butter, if you prefer.
However, it contains some
transfats so I prefer to use
cocoa butter instead.

SUGAR-FREE CHOCOLATE

MAKES 36 CHOCOLATES

80 g cocoa butter (available from
   health food stores), chopped
⅓ cup cocoa powder, sifted

Dextrose syrup
1 cup dextrose
1 cup water

Making your own chocolate at home is easier than you
might think, especially if you have your own chocolate
moulds. I encourage you to give this a go – you will
never miss bought chocolate again.

1   To make the dextrose syrup, put the dextrose and water into
    a small saucepan and stir over medium heat until the dextrose
    has dissolved and the mixture is well combined. (Makes about
    1 cup. Store any leftover syrup in an airtight container in the
    fridge for up to 1 month.)

2   Put the cocoa butter into a heatproof bowl over a saucepan of
    boiling water and stir until melted. Add the cocoa and ¼ cup
    of the dextrose syrup and stir until melted and well combined.

3   Pour the chocolate mixture into tablespoon-sized chocolate
    moulds. Refrigerate for 2-3 hours or until set. Store in an
    airtight container in the fridge for up to 2 weeks.

» VARIATION:
   You can use glucose syrup instead
   of homemade dextrose syrup,
   if you prefer.

GREEK EASTER BISCUITS

MAKES ABOUT 16

250 g unsalted butter, chopped and softened

½ cup dextrose, plus extra for dusting

2 teaspoons ground allspice

1 teaspoon vanilla essence, or to taste

2½ cups plain flour, sifted

½ cup ground almonds

This traditional Greek Easter treat is a great sweet alternative for when everyone has had enough chocolate!

1 Beat the butter, dextrose, allspice and vanilla with an electric mixer and until light and creamy. Fold in the flour and ground almonds until well combined. Wrap in plastic film and refrigerate for 30 minutes.

2 Preheat the oven to 160°C (140°C fan-forced). Line 2 baking trays with baking paper.

3 Working with 2 tablespoonfuls of the dough at a time, roll into a short log, then bend slightly to make a crescent shape. Put onto the prepared trays.

4 Bake the biscuits for 20 minutes or until firm. Dust to coat in the extra dextrose while still warm. Transfer to a wire rack to cool. These are best eaten on the day they are made.

GRAVEYARD HALLOWEEN CAKES

MAKES 12

90 g unsalted butter, chopped
  and softened

1½ cups dextrose

1 teaspoon vanilla essence,
  or to taste

3 eggs

1½ cups self-raising flour, sifted

⅓ cup cocoa powder, sifted

¾ cup milk

Chocolate fudge icing

1½ cups dextrose

½ cup cocoa powder, sifted

100 g unsalted butter, chopped
  and softened

½ cup milk

1 tablespoon vanilla essence,
  or to taste

The kids will love decorating these cakes with 'dirt' (chocolate cake crumbs) and novelty Halloween items! If trick-or-treating has become a tradition in your neighbourhood and you don't want to hand out lollies, make these instead.

1 Preheat the oven to 180°C (160°C fan-forced). Line a 12-hole muffin tin with paper cases.

2 Beat the butter, dextrose and vanilla with an electric mixer until light and creamy. Add one egg at a time, beating well after adding each one.

3 Add the flour, cocoa and milk and continue to beat until just combined. Spoon the batter evenly into the prepared paper cases.

4 Bake the cakes for 25–30 minutes or until cooked when tested with a skewer. Transfer to a wire rack to cool completely.

5 Use a tablespoon to scoop out the centre of each cupcake, leaving a 1 cm border. Pulse the scooped-out cake in a food processor to form small crumbs. Set aside.

6 To make the icing, beat the dextrose, cocoa and butter with an electric mixer for 2 minutes. Add the milk and vanilla and continue to beat for 3–5 minutes or until the mixture is light and fluffy.

7 Spread a little of the chocolate fudge icing in the scooped out centre of each cupcake. Decorate with cake crumbs and Halloween items, if desired. These are best eaten on the day they are made.

GINGERBREAD

MAKES ABOUT 24

2 cups plain flour
2 teaspoons ground ginger
1 teaspoon ground cinnamon
½ teaspoon ground nutmeg
¼ teaspoon baking powder
110 g unsalted butter, chopped
and softened
½ cup dextrose
⅓ cup glucose syrup
1 egg
1 quantity Egg-white Icing
(see page 192)

》 VARIATION:

If you wish to use these to
decorate your Christmas tree,
use a 1 cm piping nozzle to
make a hole in the top of
each piece of dough before
the biscuits are baked. Run
a skewer around each hole
just after the biscuits come
out of the oven to ensure it
has a smooth edge for
threading. Thread onto your
choice of festive ribbons.

Wrapped in cellophane, these beautifully spiced biscuits
make a lovely edible Christmas gift.

1   Sift the flour, ginger, cinnamon, nutmeg and baking powder
into a large bowl.

2   Beat the butter and dextrose with an electric mixer until light
and creamy. Add the glucose and egg and continue to beat for
2–3 minutes. With the motor on low speed, add the flour
mixture and beat until the dough just comes together. Gently
press together to form a disc, then wrap in plastic film and
refrigerate for 30 minutes.

3   Preheat the oven to 180°C (160°C fan-forced). Line 2 baking
trays with baking paper.

4   Divide the dough in half. Place one half at a time in between
2 sheets of baking paper and roll until 3 mm thick. Put each
piece of dough into the freezer for 10 minutes. Use a gingerbread man, angel, star or other Christmas-themed cookie
cutter to cut out shapes. Place the shapes on the prepared
baking trays.

5   Bake the biscuits for 10–12 minutes or until golden. Leave to
cool completely on the trays.

6   Put the icing into a piping bag fitted with a 5 mm nozzle, then
ice the biscuits as desired. Set aside for 2 hours or until the icing
has set. Store leftover gingerbread in an airtight container for up
to 2 days.

CHRISTMAS SUMMER PUDDING

SERVES 6

250 g strawberries

250 g raspberries

250 g blueberries

½ cup dextrose

1 teaspoon vanilla extract,
or to taste

¼ cup water

olive oil spray, for greasing

8 slices wholemeal bread,
crusts removed

mixed berries (optional) and
Custard (see page 192),
to serve

A traditional Christmas pudding isn't quite the same without the dried fruit, so if a steamed pudding is what you're after try adding ground ginger to the toffee puddings on page 114. Alternatively, I like this quick, light and refreshing chilled summer pudding – perfect (and more suited) for a hot Australian Christmas day. Add a splash of brandy to the custard, if you like, to make it even more festive.

1 Put the strawberries, raspberries, blueberries, dextrose, vanilla and water into a medium saucepan. Cook, stirring frequently, over medium heat for 3–4 minutes or until the dextrose has dissolved. Strain over a bowl, reserving the liquid.

2 Lightly spray a 1 litre-capacity pudding bowl with olive oil spray.

3 Cut the bread slices in half, then dip 12 pieces into the reserved liquid and use to line the base and side of the pudding bowl. Spoon the berry mixture into the centre of the bowl. Dip the remaining 4 bread pieces into the remaining liquid and cover the top of the berries. Wrap the pudding bowl tightly with plastic film, then weight down with a couple of tins of food and refrigerate overnight.

4 Carefully turn out the pudding from the bowl and serve with extra berries and custard, if desired.

CHRISTMAS CUPCAKES

MAKES 12

120 g unsalted butter, chopped
and softened

1 cup dextrose

2 eggs

1 teaspoon vanilla essence,
or to taste

2 cups self-raising flour, sifted

1 cup milk

Hard icing

1 cup dextrose

1 egg white

1 tablespoon warm water

You could leave half the icing white and colour half green or red, then use the white icing to create snowflake or other Christmas-themed patterns on the top of these moist little cakes.

1 Preheat the oven to 180°C (160°C fan-forced). Line a 12-hole muffin tin with paper cases.

2 Beat the butter and dextrose with an electric mixer until light and creamy. Add the eggs and vanilla and continue to beat until well combined. With the motor running, alternately add the flour and milk and beat until just combined. Spoon the batter evenly into the paper cases.

3 Bake the cakes for 15–20 minutes or until cooked when tested with a skewer. Transfer to a wire rack to cool completely.

4 To make the hard icing, whisk together the dextrose, egg white and water until smooth. Spread onto the cooled cupcakes. Set aside for 2 hours or until hard.

5 Serve decorated with Christmas-themed decorations, if desired. Store leftover cakes individually wrapped in plastic film or freezer bags in an airtight container in the freezer for up to 2 weeks.

ANGEL COOKIES

MAKES ABOUT 22

250 g unsalted butter, chopped and softened

1 cup dextrose, plus extra for dusting

1 egg yolk

2 teaspoons vanilla essence, or to taste

2 cups plain flour, sifted

Thread these pretty cookies onto ribbon and use to decorate your Christmas tree.

1 Beat the butter and dextrose with an electric mixer for 8-10 minutes or until light and creamy. Add the egg yolk and vanilla and beat to combine. Add the flour and beat until a smooth dough forms. Gently press together to form a disc, then wrap in plastic film and refrigerate for 30 minutes.

2 Preheat the oven to 180°C (160°C fan-forced). Line 2 baking trays with baking paper.

3 Roll out the dough between 2 sheets of baking paper until 5 mm thick. Use a 7 cm angel cookie cutter to cut out cookies and place on the prepared trays. Use a 1 cm piping nozzle to make a hole in the top of each cookie (the hole for hanging needs to be made before the biscuits are baked). Place the dough on the prepared baking trays.

4 Bake the biscuits for 8-10 minutes or until golden. Run a skewer around each hole just after the biscuits have come out of the oven to ensure it has a smooth edge for threading. Leave to cool for 10 minutes on the trays. Sprinkle with extra dextrose. Transfer to wire racks and leave to cool completely. Store in an airtight container for up to 5 days.

SPICED CHRISTMAS CAKE

MAKES 4 SMALL CAKES OR 1 LARGE CAKE

225 g unsalted butter, chopped and softened

½ cup dextrose

4 eggs

1¼ cups self-raising flour, sifted

1 tablespoon mixed spice

1 teaspoon ground ginger

½ teaspoon ground cloves

1 tablespoon finely grated lemon zest

1 tablespoon finely grated orange zest

1 tablespoon rice malt syrup

2 tablespoons brandy

1 quantity Almond Brittle (see page 191) and cream, to serve (optional)

This moist spiced cake is baked in a large square cake tin and can either be served as one large cake or cut into four to make smaller cakes to give as gifts.

1 Preheat the oven to 180°C (160°C fan-forced). Grease and line a 20 cm square cake tin with baking paper.

2 Beat the butter and dextrose with an electric mixer until light and creamy. Add one egg at a time, beating well after adding each one. Add the flour, mixed spice, ginger, cloves, lemon zest, orange zest, rice malt syrup and brandy and beat until just combined.

3 Spoon the batter into the prepared tin and smooth the top with the back of a wet spoon. Wrap the outside of the tin with 2 layers of brown paper and secure with kitchen string.

4 Bake the cake for 2 hours or until cooked when tested with a skewer. Cool in the tin for 5 minutes, then turn out onto a wire rack to cool completely.

5 If you wish to make 4 individual cakes, then cut the cake into 4 even squares. Top with almond brittle and serve with cream, if desired. (Alternatively, wrap individually to give as Christmas gifts or freeze for up to 2 weeks.)

EGG NOG PANNA COTTA

SERVES 6

3½ cups milk
1 cup thickened cream
5 egg yolks
1 cup dextrose
2 tablespoons rum
1 teaspoon ground nutmeg
1 teaspoon mixed spice
1 tablespoon powdered gelatine
Gingerbread (see page 175),
   dusted with dextrose,
   to serve (optional)

Prepare this lovely dessert in advance for Christmas to make things easier for you on the day. If you've also made gingerbread, serve them with the panna cotta to add a little crunch. Here the gingerbread dough has been cut into circles and stars, but you can use any shaped cutter you like.

1   Bring the milk and cream just to the boil in a medium saucepan over medium heat. Whisk the egg yolks and dextrose in a bowl until pale and creamy. Gradually whisk in the warm milk mixture.

2   Transfer the mixture to a clean saucepan, then cook over low heat for 3-4 minutes or until the mixture is thick enough to coat the back of a spoon.

3   Remove from the heat, then stir in the rum, nutmeg and mixed spice and cool to room temperature. Meanwhile, lightly grease six ½ cup-capacity pudding moulds, glasses or ramekins.

4   Place ½ cup of the egg nog in a small jug, then sprinkle over the gelatine and mix until well combined. Stir into the remaining egg nog mixture, then transfer to a clean saucepan. Cook over medium heat, stirring gently until the gelatine has dissolved. Strain the mixture evenly into the prepared moulds. Refrigerate for 4 hours or until set.

5   Turn out the panna cotta and serve, topped with gingerbread dusted with dextrose, if you like.

BAS

ICS

ROASTED STRAWBERRY & RHUBARB JAM

MAKES ABOUT 3 CUPS

500 g strawberries, hulled
    and quartered

500 g rhubarb stalks,
    roughly chopped

2 teaspoons vanilla essence,
    or to taste

2 cups dextrose

1 tablespoon lemon juice

This easy jam will really thicken as it cools in the fridge.
It's great spread on pancakes (see page 8), scones (see
page 15) or coconut bread (see page 16).

1   Preheat the oven to 180°C (160°C fan-forced).

2   Mix the strawberries, rhubarb, vanilla, dextrose and lemon juice
    in a bowl until combined. Transfer to a baking dish and cover
    tightly with foil. Roast for 30 minutes, then remove the foil and
    roast for another 20–30 minutes or until thickened. Transfer to
    sterilised jars (see below) and leave to cool completely. Store in
    the fridge for up to 1 week.

- - - - - - - - - - - - - - - -

» TIP:

To lengthen the shelf life of your
jam it is important to sterilise
the storage jars. Preheat the
oven to 110°C (90°C fan-forced).
Put the clean jars and lids into
a deep saucepan and cover
with water. Boil for 10 minutes.
Carefully transfer to a baking
tray lined with a clean tea
towel and heat in the oven
for 15 minutes.

HOT CHOCOLATE FUDGE SAUCE

MAKES ABOUT ½ CUP

30 g unsalted butter
2 tablespoons cocoa powder
⅓ cup dextrose
½ cup thickened cream
1 teaspoon vanilla essence,
   or to taste

1 Put the butter, cocoa, dextrose, cream and vanilla into a heatproof bowl over a saucepan of simmering water, making sure the bottom of the bowl doesn't touch the water. Heat until melted and well combined. Refrigerate for 30 minutes or until thickened slightly. Heat gently in a small saucepan over low heat, then serve warm.

ALMOND BRITTLE

MAKES ABOUT 1½ CUPS

1 cup dextrose
½ cup blanched almonds

1 Put the dextrose into a large non-stick frying pan and cook over medium heat for 4-5 minutes or until melted and golden. Pour onto a baking tray lined with baking paper, sprinkle over the almonds and leave to cool for 10 minutes or until crisp. Break into large pieces. Store in an airtight container for up to 3 days.

CUSTARD

SERVES 4

1 cup milk
1 cup thickened cream
1 vanilla bean, split and seeds scraped
5 egg yolks
1 cup dextrose

1   Put the milk, cream and vanilla into
    a medium saucepan. Bring just to the
    boil over medium heat.

2   Whisk the egg yolks and dextrose in a medium
    bowl until thick and pale. Gradually whisk in the
    milk mixture until well combined. Transfer to
    a clean saucepan and cook over medium heat,
    stirring for 4-6 minutes or until thickened.
    Strain the mixture through a fine-mesh sieve
    and serve warm or cold.

» VARIATION:
    Add a little brandy to serve with your
    Christmas cake or pudding.

EGG-WHITE ICING

MAKES ENOUGH TO ICE 12 CUPCAKES
OR 24 BISCUITS

1 cup dextrose
2 egg whites
1 tablespoon warm water

1   Whisk together the dextrose, egg whites
    and water until smooth. Use to decorate
    your cake/s or biscuits.

POACHED CHERRIES

MAKES ABOUT 3 CUPS

1 cup dextrose
1 cup water
400 g cherries, stems removed, pitted

1   Put the dextrose and water into a small
    saucepan. Stir over medium heat until the
    dextrose has dissolved. Add the cherries
    and simmer for 5 minutes or until the syrup
    has thickened slightly but the cherries still
    hold their shape. Set aside to cool. Store in
    an airtight container in the fridge for up to
    3 days.

PASSIONFRUIT CURD

MAKES ABOUT 1½ CUPS

2 eggs
2 egg yolks
1 cup dextrose
80 g cold unsalted butter, chopped
4 ripe passionfruit, halved and pulp removed

1 Put the eggs, yolks and dextrose into a medium saucepan and whisk over low heat until smooth. Add the butter and passionfruit pulp and whisk continuously for 8–10 minutes or until thickened. Strain through a fine-mesh sieve. Cover closely with plastic film and cool completely. Store in a sterilised glass jar (see page 190) in the fridge for up to 1 week.

LEMON CURD

MAKES ABOUT 1½ CUPS

2 eggs
2 egg yolks
1 cup dextrose
80 g cold unsalted butter, chopped
finely grated zest and juice of 2 lemons

1 Put the eggs, yolks and dextrose into a medium saucepan and whisk over low heat until smooth. Add the butter and lemon zest and juice and whisk continuously for 8–10 minutes or until thickened. Strain through a fine-mesh sieve. Cover closely with plastic film and cool completely. Store in a sterilised glass jar (see page 190) in the fridge for up to 1 week.

HOMEMADE TOMATO SAUCE

MAKES 1 LITRE

2 kg ripe tomatoes,
   roughly chopped
1 onion, roughly chopped
2 cloves garlic, crushed
2 teaspoons black peppercorns
2 teaspoons mustard seeds
2 cloves
1 teaspoon smoked paprika
½ teaspoon ground chilli
1 cinnamon stick
⅓ cup dextrose
⅓ cup apple cider vinegar
1 tablespoon lemon juice
1 teaspoon sea salt

If you can't live without splashing tomato sauce onto your snags or meat pie, make your own with this sugar-free version.

1 Put the tomato, onion, garlic, peppercorns, mustard seeds, cloves, paprika, chilli and cinnamon into a large saucepan and bring to the boil over high heat. Reduce the heat to medium and simmer for 45–50 minutes or until reduced by half. Cool. Remove the cinnamon stick.

2 Process the mixture in a food processor until smooth. Push through a fine-mesh sieve into a clean saucepan. Add the dextrose, vinegar, lemon juice and salt and bring to the boil over high heat. Reduce the heat to medium and simmer for 15 minutes or until thickened slightly. Pour into sterilised jars or bottles (see page 190), then seal. Cool completely.

TOMATO PIZZA SAUCE

MAKES ABOUT 3 CUPS

1 kg roma tomatoes, halved
2 red onions, cut into thin wedges
2 cloves garlic, unpeeled
2 tablespoons olive oil
sea salt and freshly ground
   black pepper

Make batches of this when tomatoes are in season over the summer months, so you have a ready supply when a pizza craving strikes.

1   Preheat the oven to 180°C (160°C fan-forced).

2   Put the tomatoes, onion and garlic onto a baking tray. Drizzle with the olive oil and season with salt and pepper. Roast for 1 hour, then leave to cool slightly. Peel the garlic, discarding the skins.

3   Blend all the ingredients in a food processor until smooth. Transfer to an airtight container and refrigerate until cold. Store in the fridge for up to 2 days or freezer for up to 3 months.

HOMEMADE BARBECUE SAUCE

MAKES ABOUT 2 CUPS

2 tablespoons olive oil
1 small onion, roughly chopped
2 cloves garlic, crushed
1 fresh long red chilli, chopped
1 × 400 g tin chopped tomato
(no added sugar)
2 tablespoons tomato puree
(I use Ardmona rich and thick)
2 tablespoons dextrose
1 tablespoon worcestershire sauce
2 tablespoons white wine vinegar
1 tablespoon dijon mustard
1 tablespoon smoked paprika

Store-bought barbecue sauce contains more sugar than tomato sauce, so make this homemade sugar-free one instead. This smoky condiment also doubles as an excellent marinade for pork ribs destined for the barbecue.

1 Heat the oil in a saucepan over low heat. Add the onion and cook for 5 minutes or until slightly softened. Add the garlic, chilli, tomato, tomato puree, dextrose, worcestershire sauce, vinegar, mustard and paprika and bring to the boil. Reduce the heat to medium and simmer, stirring frequently for 25-30 minutes until thickened. Set aside to cool slightly.

2 Transfer to a blender and blend until smooth. Store in a sterilised glass jar or bottle (see page 191) in the fridge for up to 2 weeks.

SWEET CHILLI SAUCE

MAKES 1 LITRE

500 g long fresh red chillies,
  stems removed
3 cloves garlic, peeled
3 cups white vinegar
3 cups dextrose

Thanks to this recipe, there is no need to ever miss bottled sweet chilli sauce again. Add the sauce to any meat, chicken or vegetable stir-fry for an instant Thai feast at home.

1   Process the chillies in a food processor until roughly chopped. Add the garlic and 1 cup of the vinegar. Process until finely chopped.

2   Transfer the chilli mixture to a large saucepan, then add the dextrose and remaining vinegar. Cook, stirring frequently, over low heat for 5 minutes or until the dextrose has dissolved.

3   Increase the heat to high and bring to the boil. Reduce the heat to medium and simmer, stirring occasionally, for 35–40 minutes or until thickened. Transfer to sterilised glass jars (see page 190) or bottles, then store in the fridge for up to 2 weeks.

- - - - - - - - - - - - - - - - - - -

» VARIATION:
  If you like really spicy food, use small red chillies for extra heat.

ACKNOWLEDGEMENTS

Gosh it's easy to write a cookbook. Well, it's easy if your primary role is 'quality control', and all the actual work is done by seasoned professionals and your slave-driven wife. My name is on the front cover, but this book is definitely a collaboration of the very best in the business. Because I did practically nothing (other than eat pudding on a regular basis), all the author proceeds from the sale of this book are being donated to charity. My agent, Frank Stranges (who did even less than me) is also generously donating his share of the proceeds.

Peta Dent is a chef, and was responsible for designing, testing and retesting the recipes in this book. She brings an enormous wealth of cooking knowledge to the table (or should that be oven?). And besides being a consummate professional, she was an absolute delight to work with.

Vanessa Austin is the stylist responsible for making everything look gorgeous. Unlike our kids, she can make a messy spoon look like art, and she has an impeccable eye for choosing exactly the right plate to go with every single recipe. She also served as our full-sugar guinea pig at the photo shoot. Her died-in-the-wool sweet tooth meant we could get an accurate feel for how your average sugar addict would react to these dextrose-based recipes. And since a major point of this book is to give you something to feed to guests, it was important to know they wouldn't turn their noses up at any of the sweet offerings here.

Ben Dearnley clicked the button after Vanessa did the work. Not exactly, but that's how the story went at the shoot. Ben has turned out truly edible photographs. It's incredible that he can convey how the food will taste in a medium that doesn't let you smell it. I've tried, and failed, to make food look as good as Ben has managed to.

My visionary publisher, Julie Gibbs, commissioned the book – thanks Julie for continuing to champion my message. Katrina O'Brien had to find creative ways to post lamingtons and cakes across the country and deliver something that our kids were prepared to 'test', as well as making sure we delivered a book you could actually use. Kathleen Gandy edited the book and had to juggle endless alterations to the recipes with layouts, colours and extra notes about how safe some ingredients are or aren't. Emily O'Neill gave us a beautiful, playful design that makes the food jump off the page. And they all did it with grace and efficiency.

She's not on the payroll, but my wife, Lizzie, deserves special acknowledgement. Some of the recipes were developed entirely by her over years of trial and error (which was necessary because her husband banned half the contents of the supermarket). But even with the recipes developed by Peta, Lizzie has paid fanatical attention to detail. It was not good enough to just read and check – she has personally cooked most of Peta's recipes. This is the only way she can be certain they will pass the 'anyone can do this at home' test. Her devotion to the task has been truly phenomenal.

Kids will eat this stuff and love it. The only reason I can say that with absolute certainty is that all six of our munchkins (Anthony, James, Gwen, Adam, Elizabeth and Fin) have been devoted testers of chocolate cake, ice cream and all the rest. Children eating the scrumptious foods created from these pages can thank our kids for their diligence.

I hope you enjoy cooking and sharing the recipes as much as we have.

INDEX

LANTERN

Published by the Penguin Group
Penguin Group (Australia)
    707 Collins Street, Melbourne, Victoria 3008, Australia
    (a division of Pearson Australia Group Pty Ltd)
Penguin Group (USA) Inc.
    375 Hudson Street, New York, New York 10014, USA
Penguin Group (Canada)
    90 Eglinton Avenue East, Suite 700, Toronto, Canada ON M4P 2Y3
    (a division of Pearson Penguin Canada Inc.)
Penguin Books Ltd
    80 Strand, London WC2R 0RL England
Penguin Ireland
    25 St Stephen's Green, Dublin 2, Ireland
    (a division of Penguin Books Ltd)
Penguin Books India Pvt Ltd
    11 Community Centre, Panchsheel Park, New Delhi – 110 017, India
Penguin Group (NZ)
    67 Apollo Drive, Rosedale, Auckland 0632, New Zealand
    (a division of Pearson New Zealand Ltd)
Penguin Books (South Africa) (Pty) Ltd, Rosebank Office Park, Block D,
    181 Jan Smuts Avenue, Parktown North, Johannesburg, 2196, South Africa
Penguin (Beijing) Ltd
    7F, Tower B, Jiaming Center, 27 East Third Ring Road North,
    Chaoyang District, Beijing 100020, China

Penguin Books Ltd, Registered Offices: 80 Strand, London, WC2R 0RL, England

First published by Penguin Group (Australia), 2013

10 9 8 7 6 5 4 3 2 1

Text copyright © David Gillespie 2013
Photography © Ben Dearnley 2013

Cover design by Emily O'Neill © Penguin Group (Australia)
Text design by Emily O'Neill © Penguin Group (Australia)
Styling for food and incidental photography by Vanessa Austin
Recipe development by Peta Dent

Typeset in Chaparral Pro and Interstate by Post Pre-Press Group, Brisbane, Queensland
Colour separation by Splitting Image Colour Studio, Clayton, Victoria
Printed and bound in China by South China Printing Co. Ltd

National Library of Australia
Cataloguing-in-Publication data:

9780143568261 (pbk.)
Gillespie, David.
The sweet poison quit plan cookbook / David Gillespie.
9780143568261 (pbk.)
Sugar-free diet--Recipes.
Sugar-free diet.
Cooking.

641.5638

penguin.com.au/lantern